CONTENTS

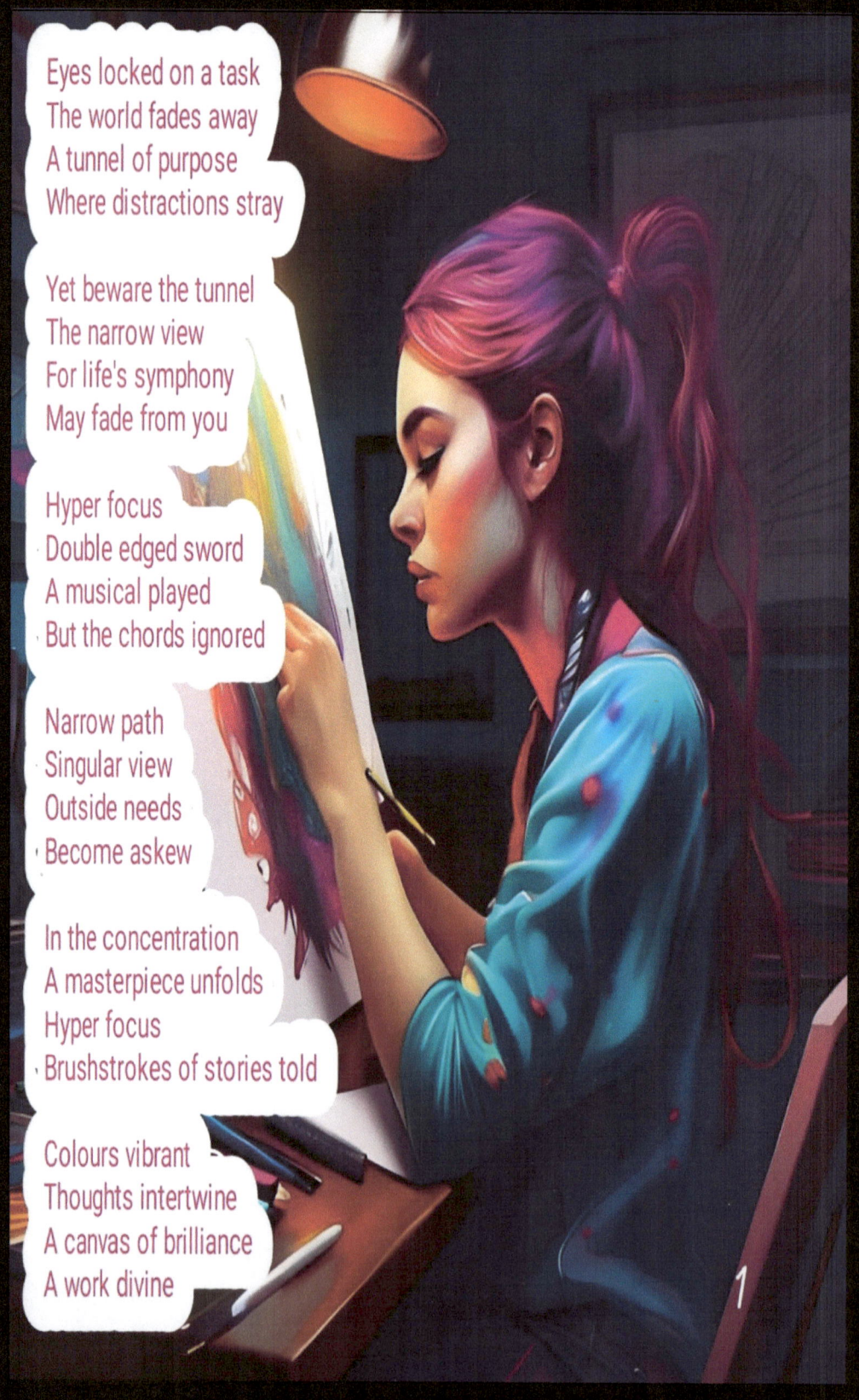

Eyes locked on a task
The world fades away
A tunnel of purpose
Where distractions stray

Yet beware the tunnel
The narrow view
For life's symphony
May fade from you

Hyper focus
Double edged sword
A musical played
But the chords ignored

Narrow path
Singular view
Outside needs
Become askew

In the concentration
A masterpiece unfolds
Hyper focus
Brushstrokes of stories told

Colours vibrant
Thoughts intertwine
A canvas of brilliance
A work divine

1

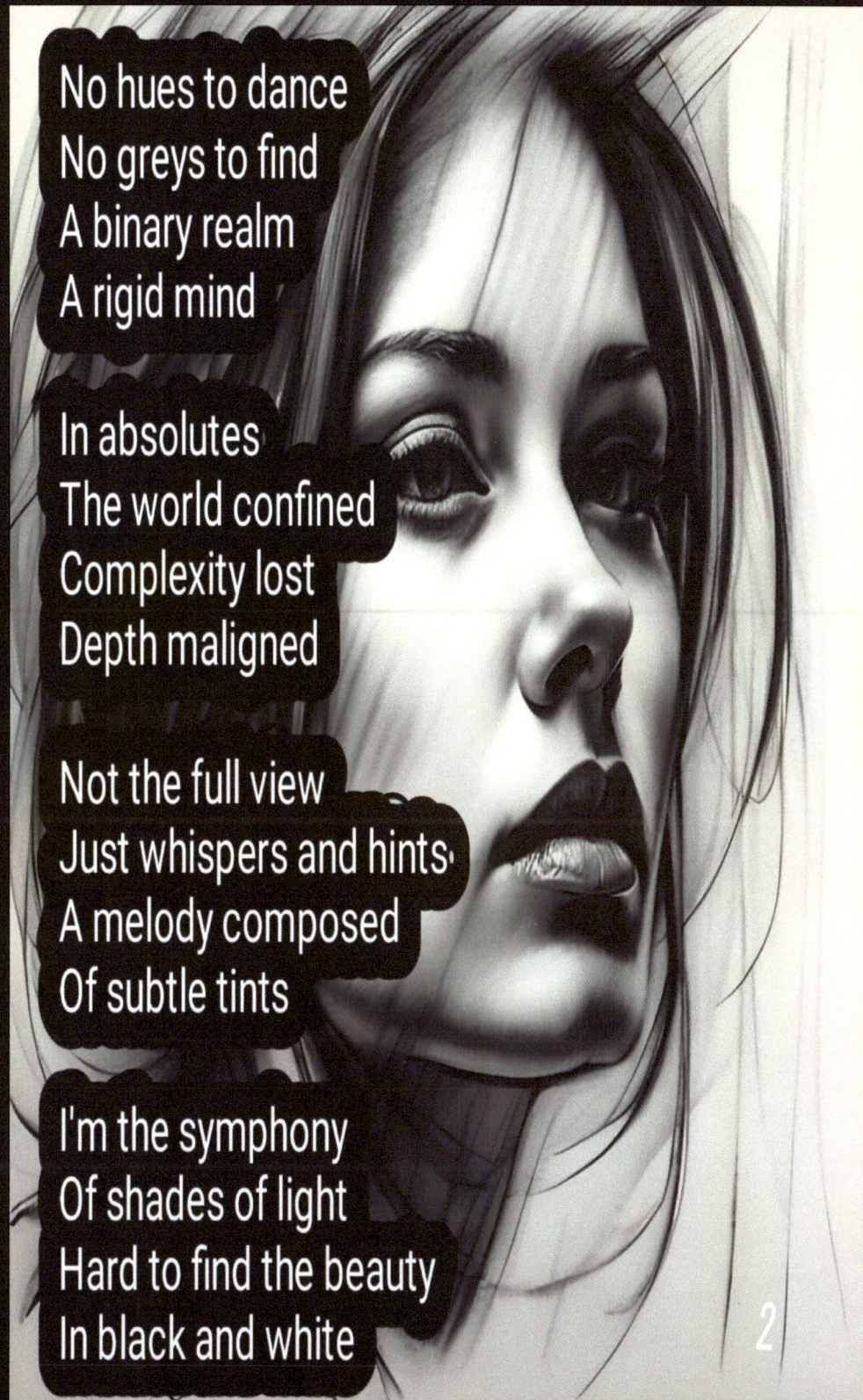

No hues to dance
No greys to find
A binary realm
A rigid mind

In absolutes
The world confined
Complexity lost
Depth maligned

Not the full view
Just whispers and hints
A melody composed
Of subtle tints

I'm the symphony
Of shades of light
Hard to find the beauty
In black and white

2

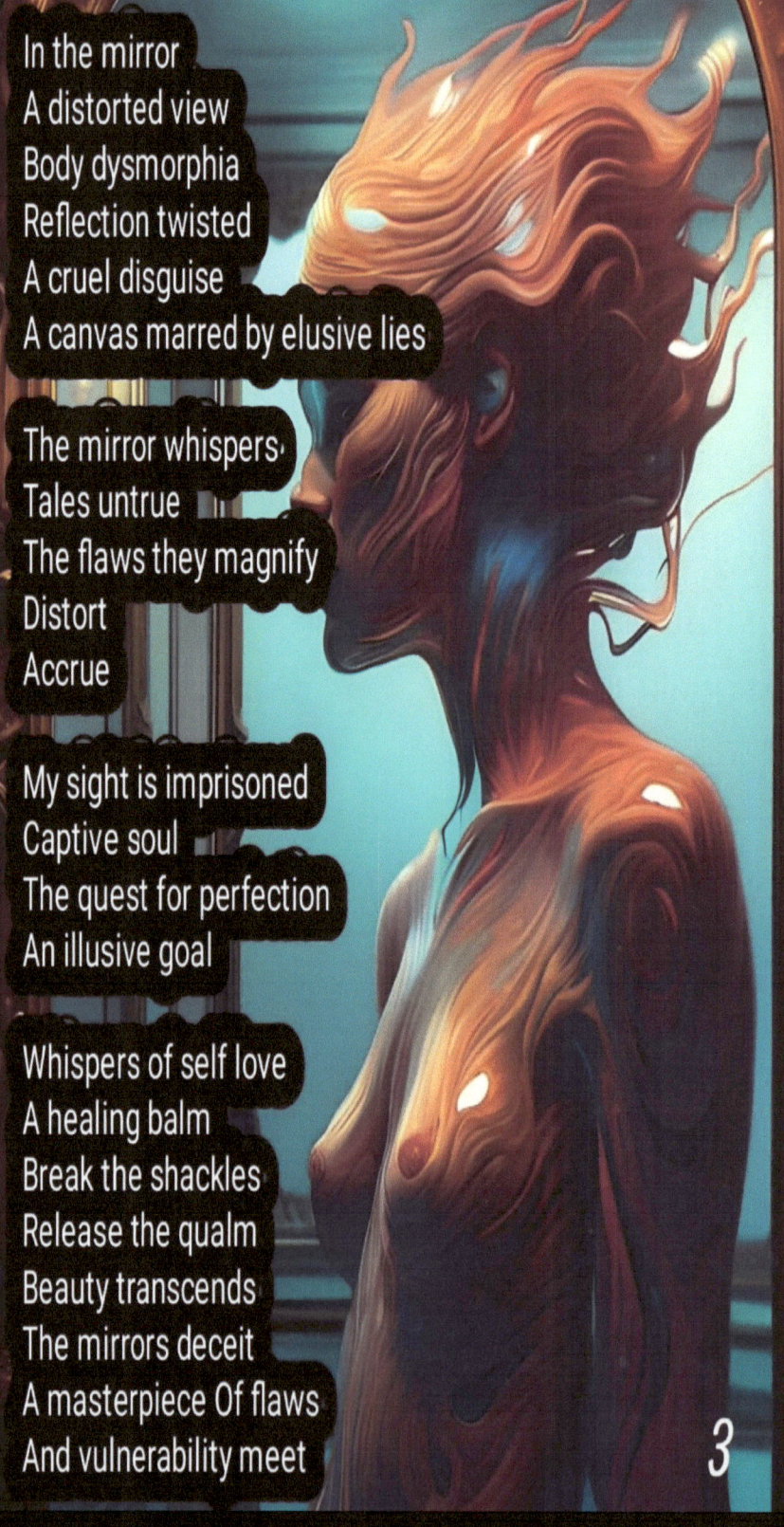

In the mirror
A distorted view
Body dysmorphia
Reflection twisted
A cruel disguise
A canvas marred by elusive lies

The mirror whispers
Tales untrue
The flaws they magnify
Distort
Accrue

My sight is imprisoned
Captive soul
The quest for perfection
An illusive goal

Whispers of self love
A healing balm
Break the shackles
Release the qualm
Beauty transcends
The mirrors deceit
A masterpiece Of flaws
And vulnerability meet

3

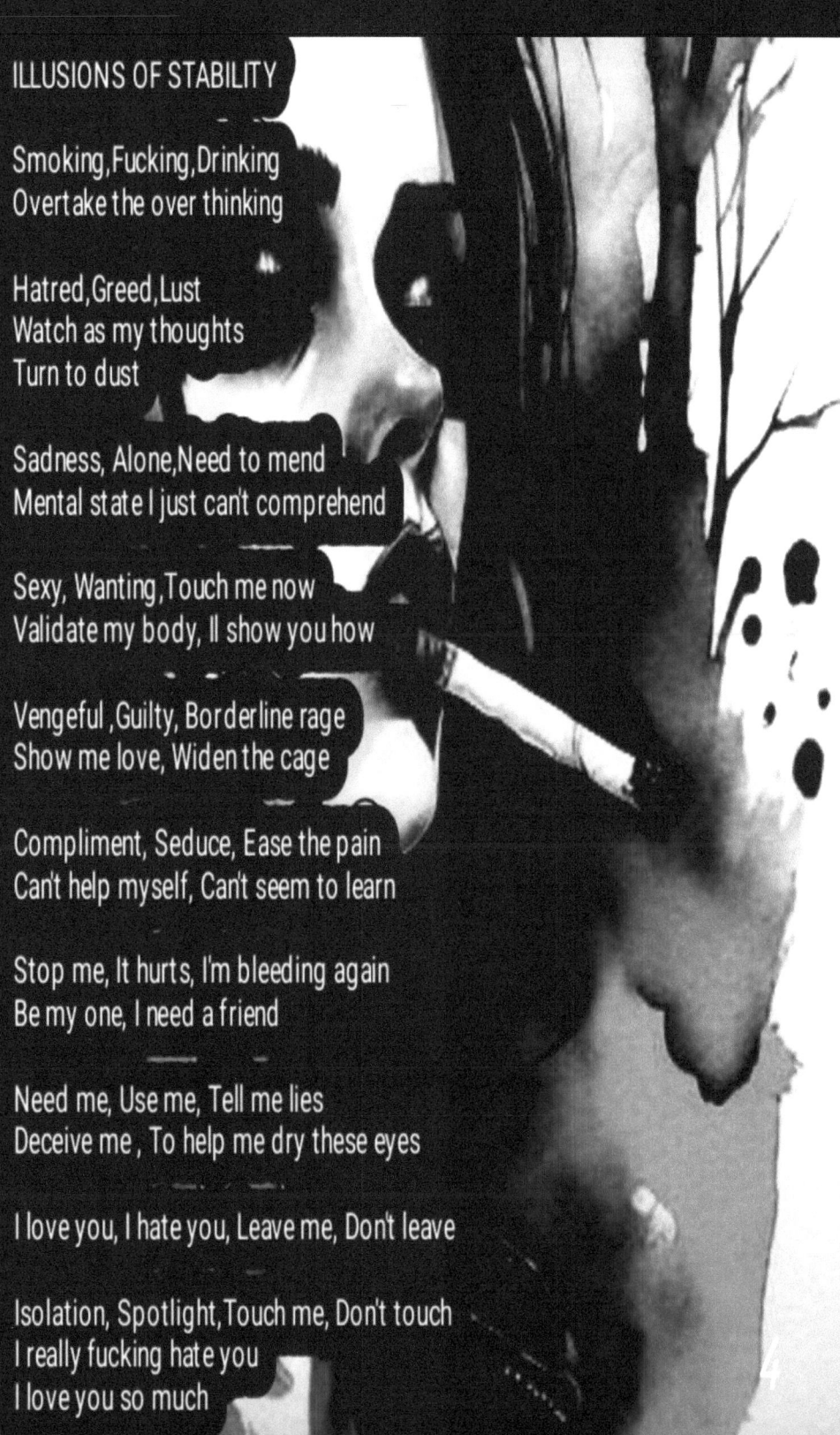

ILLUSIONS OF STABILITY

Smoking,Fucking,Drinking
Overtake the over thinking

Hatred,Greed,Lust
Watch as my thoughts
Turn to dust

Sadness, Alone,Need to mend
Mental state I just can't comprehend

Sexy, Wanting,Touch me now
Validate my body, Il show you how

Vengeful ,Guilty, Borderline rage
Show me love, Widen the cage

Compliment, Seduce, Ease the pain
Can't help myself, Can't seem to learn

Stop me, It hurts, I'm bleeding again
Be my one, I need a friend

Need me, Use me, Tell me lies
Deceive me , To help me dry these eyes

I love you, I hate you, Leave me, Don't leave

Isolation, Spotlight,Touch me, Don't touch
I really fucking hate you
I love you so much

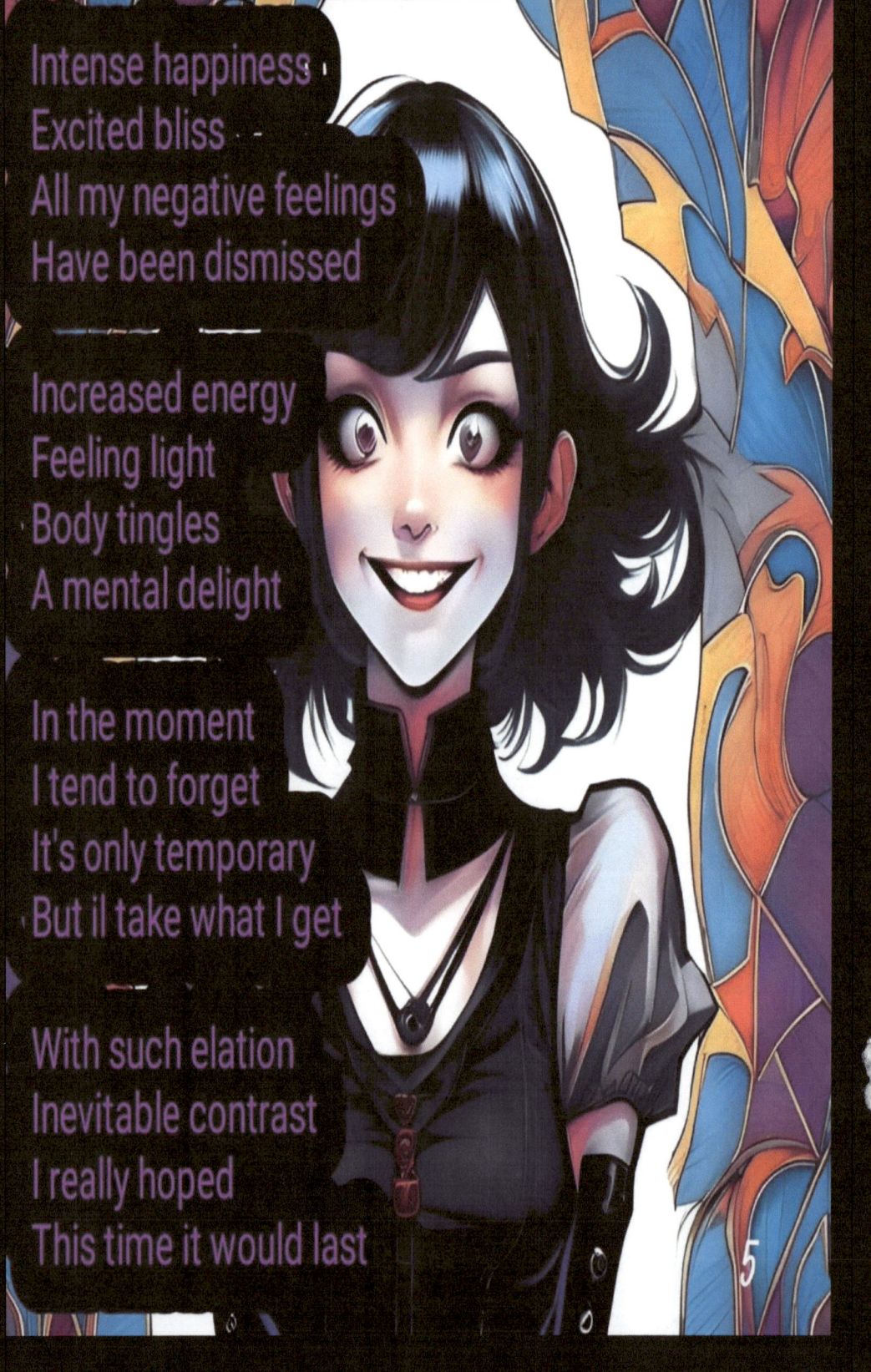

Intense happiness
Excited bliss
All my negative feelings
Have been dismissed

Increased energy
Feeling light
Body tingles
A mental delight

In the moment
I tend to forget
It's only temporary
But il take what I get

With such elation
Inevitable contrast
I really hoped
This time it would last

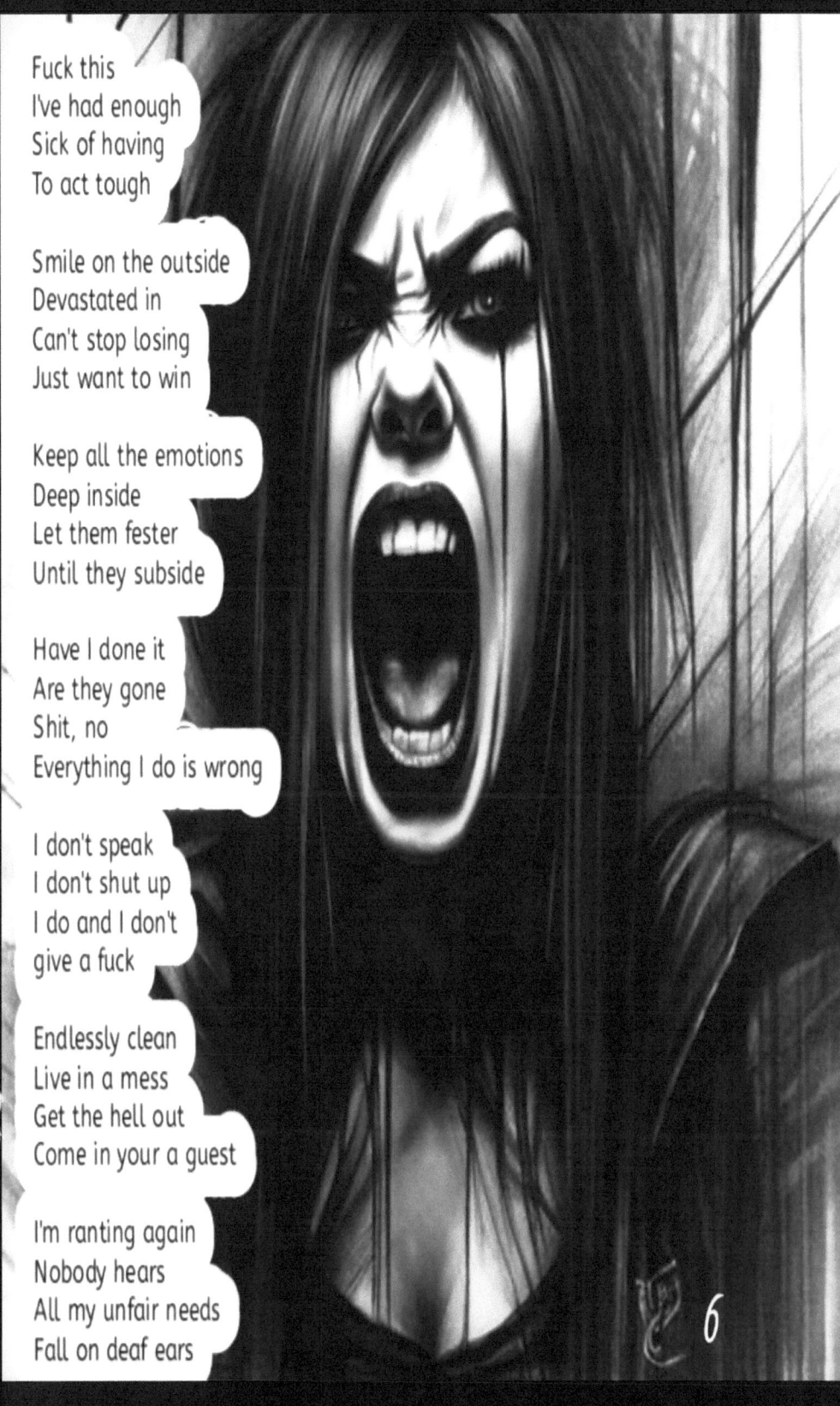

Fuck this
I've had enough
Sick of having
To act tough

Smile on the outside
Devastated in
Can't stop losing
Just want to win

Keep all the emotions
Deep inside
Let them fester
Until they subside

Have I done it
Are they gone
Shit, no
Everything I do is wrong

I don't speak
I don't shut up
I do and I don't
give a fuck

Endlessly clean
Live in a mess
Get the hell out
Come in your a guest

I'm ranting again
Nobody hears
All my unfair needs
Fall on deaf ears

6

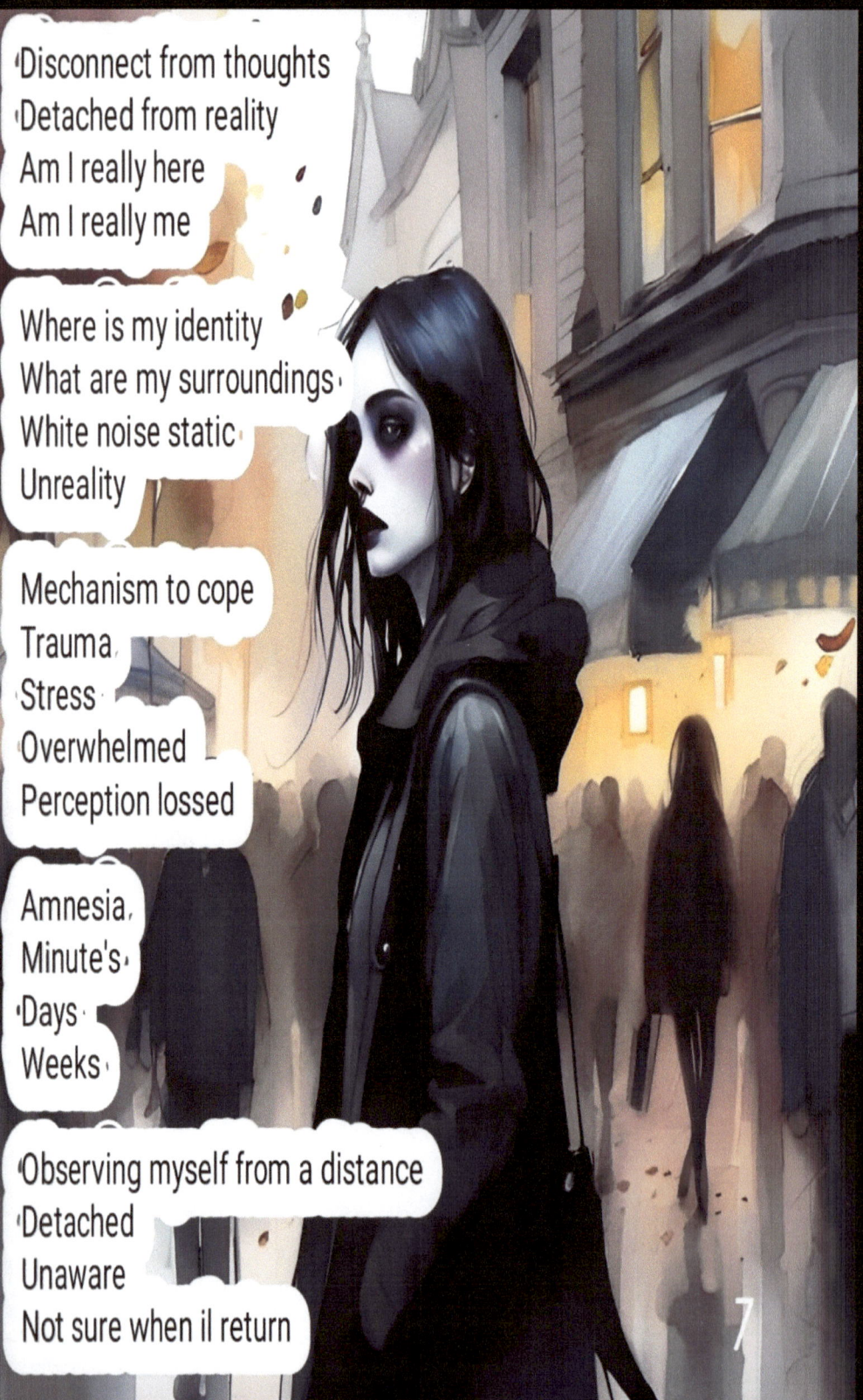

Disconnect from thoughts
Detached from reality
Am I really here
Am I really me

Where is my identity
What are my surroundings
White noise static
Unreality

Mechanism to cope
Trauma
Stress
Overwhelmed
Perception lossed

Amnesia
Minute's
Days
Weeks

Observing myself from a distance
Detached
Unaware
Not sure when il return

7

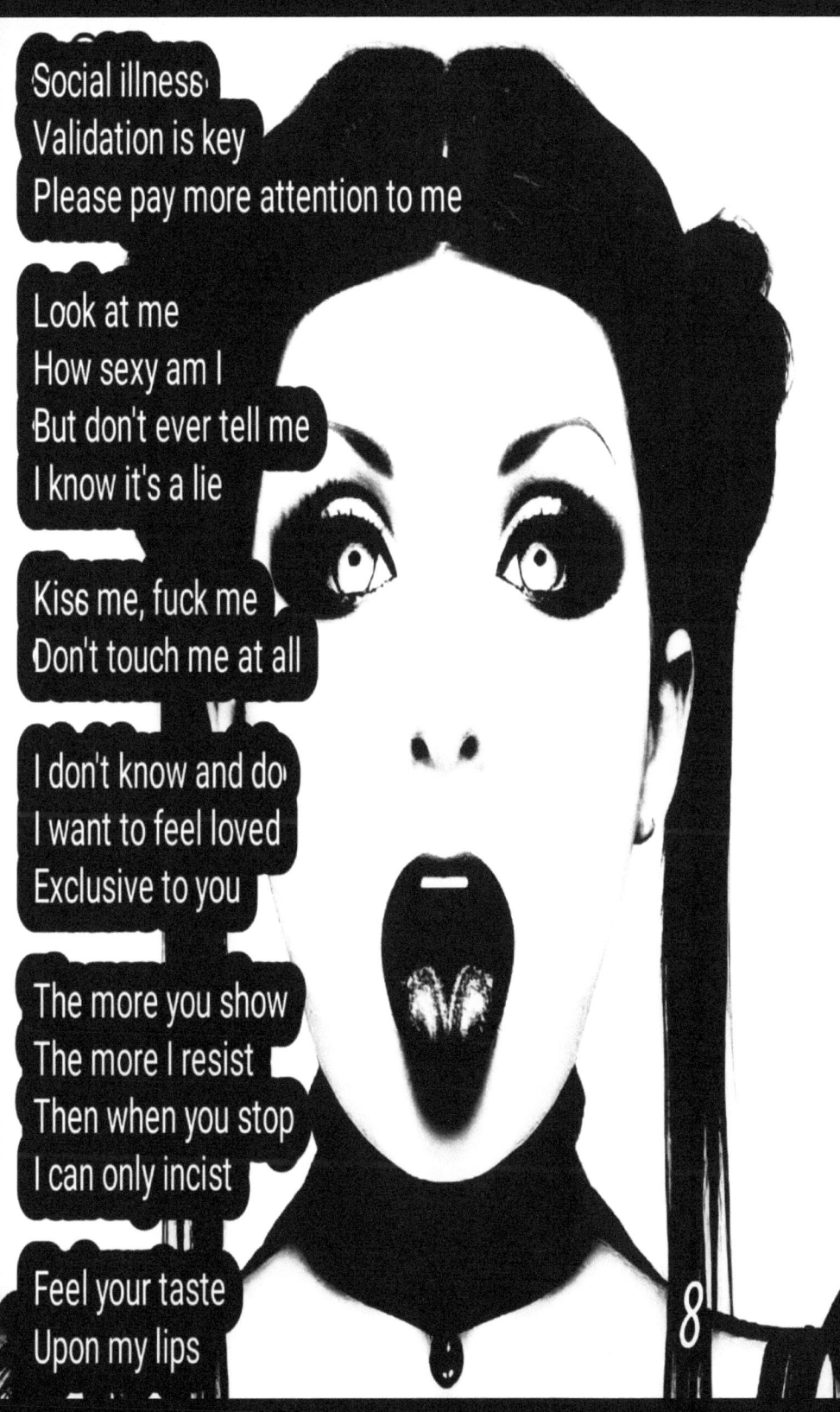

Social illness
Validation is key
Please pay more attention to me

Look at me
How sexy am I
But don't ever tell me
I know it's a lie

Kiss me, fuck me
Don't touch me at all

I don't know and do
I want to feel loved
Exclusive to you

The more you show
The more I resist
Then when you stop
I can only incist

Feel your taste
Upon my lips

It's a whirlwind
Rushing around my head
Glad to be alive
Wish I was dead

Destroy you
Make you whole
Keep you
While you play your role

Better respond
Don't be late
Put me first
Or il believe its hate

Il do anything
To get your desire
Fill your heart
With a lustfull fire

Watch me scream
Watch me beg
Until your discarded
Become the dregs

I appear to be awful
It's probably true
But when real love comes
You will be glad it's you

9

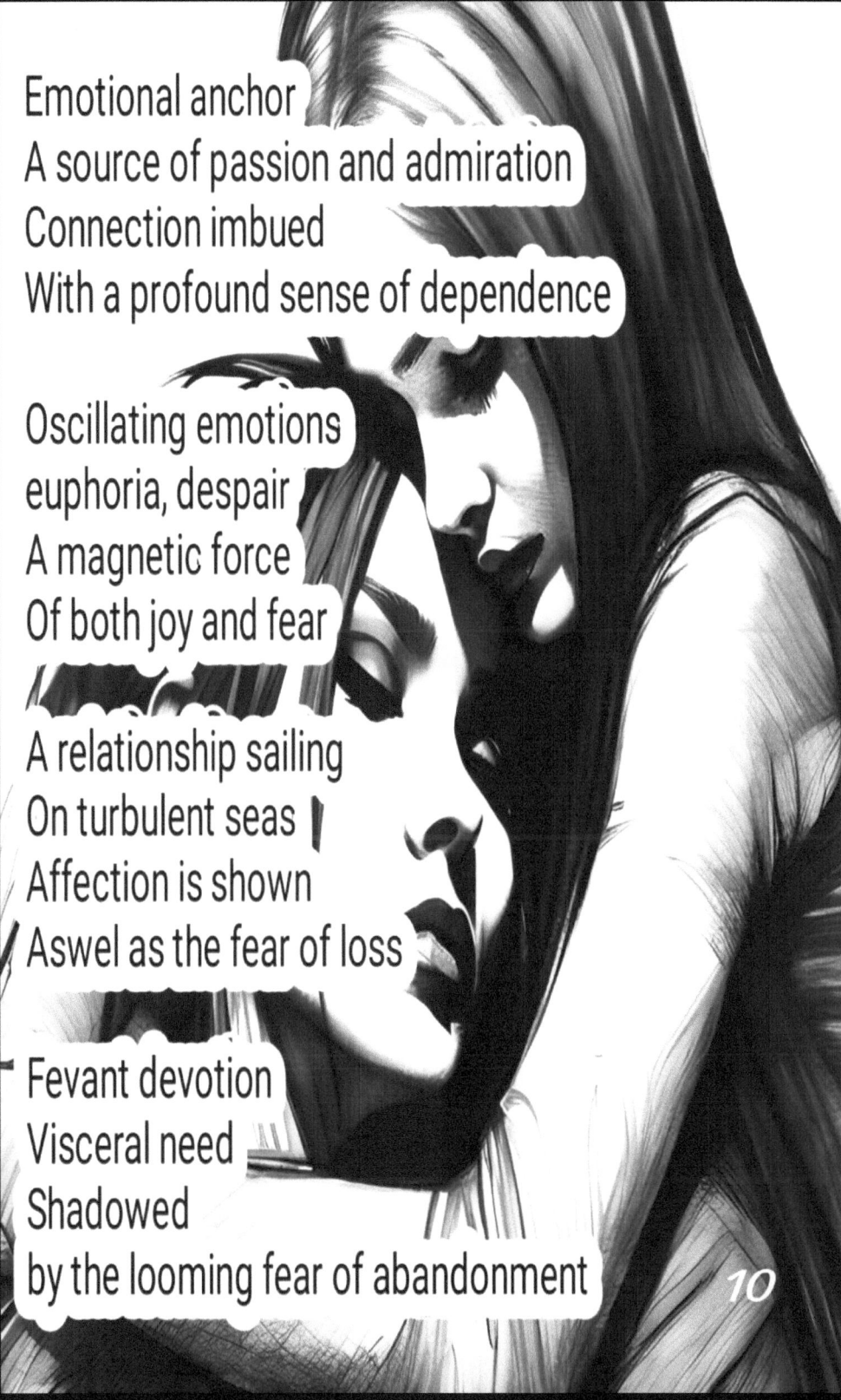

Emotional anchor
A source of passion and admiration
Connection imbued
With a profound sense of dependence

Oscillating emotions
euphoria, despair
A magnetic force
Of both joy and fear

A relationship sailing
On turbulent seas
Affection is shown
Aswel as the fear of loss

Fevant devotion
Visceral need
Shadowed
by the looming fear of abandonment

10

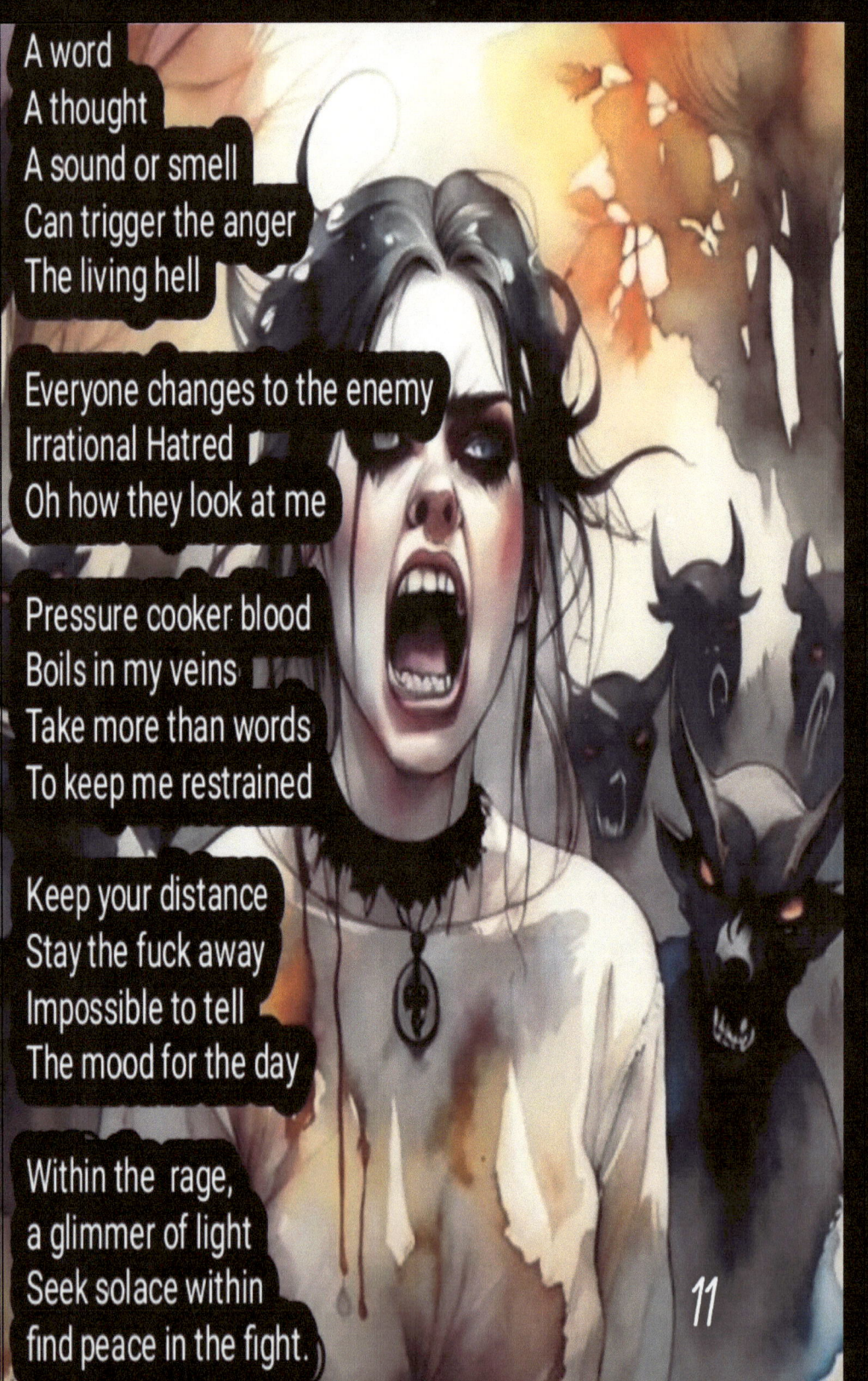

A word
A thought
A sound or smell
Can trigger the anger
The living hell

Everyone changes to the enemy
Irrational Hatred
Oh how they look at me

Pressure cooker blood
Boils in my veins
Take more than words
To keep me restrained

Keep your distance
Stay the fuck away
Impossible to tell
The mood for the day

Within the rage,
a glimmer of light
Seek solace within
find peace in the fight.

11

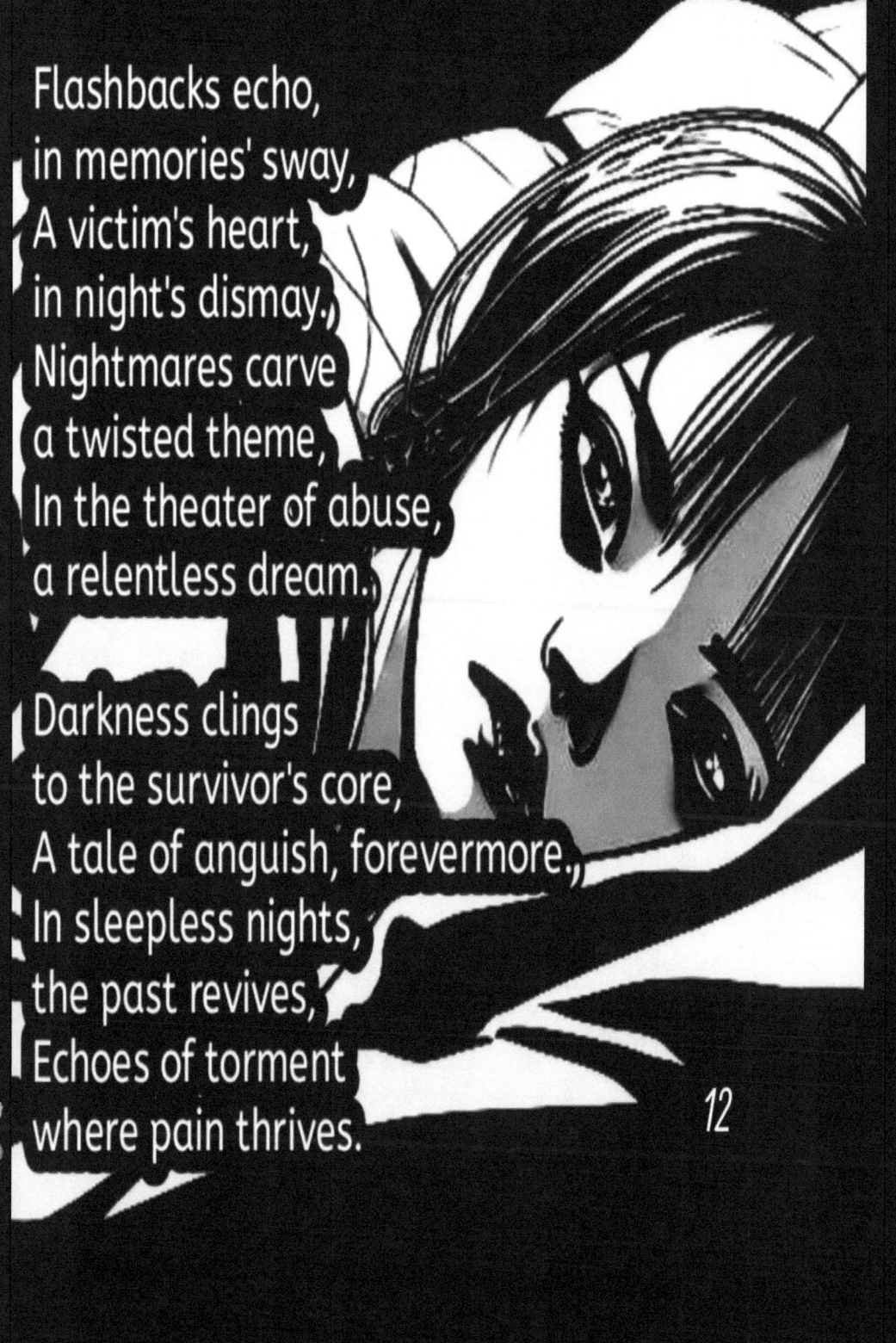

Flashbacks echo,
in memories' sway,
A victim's heart,
in night's dismay,
Nightmares carve
a twisted theme,
In the theater of abuse,
a relentless dream.

Darkness clings
to the survivor's core,
A tale of anguish, forevermore,
In sleepless nights,
the past revives,
Echoes of torment
where pain thrives.

12

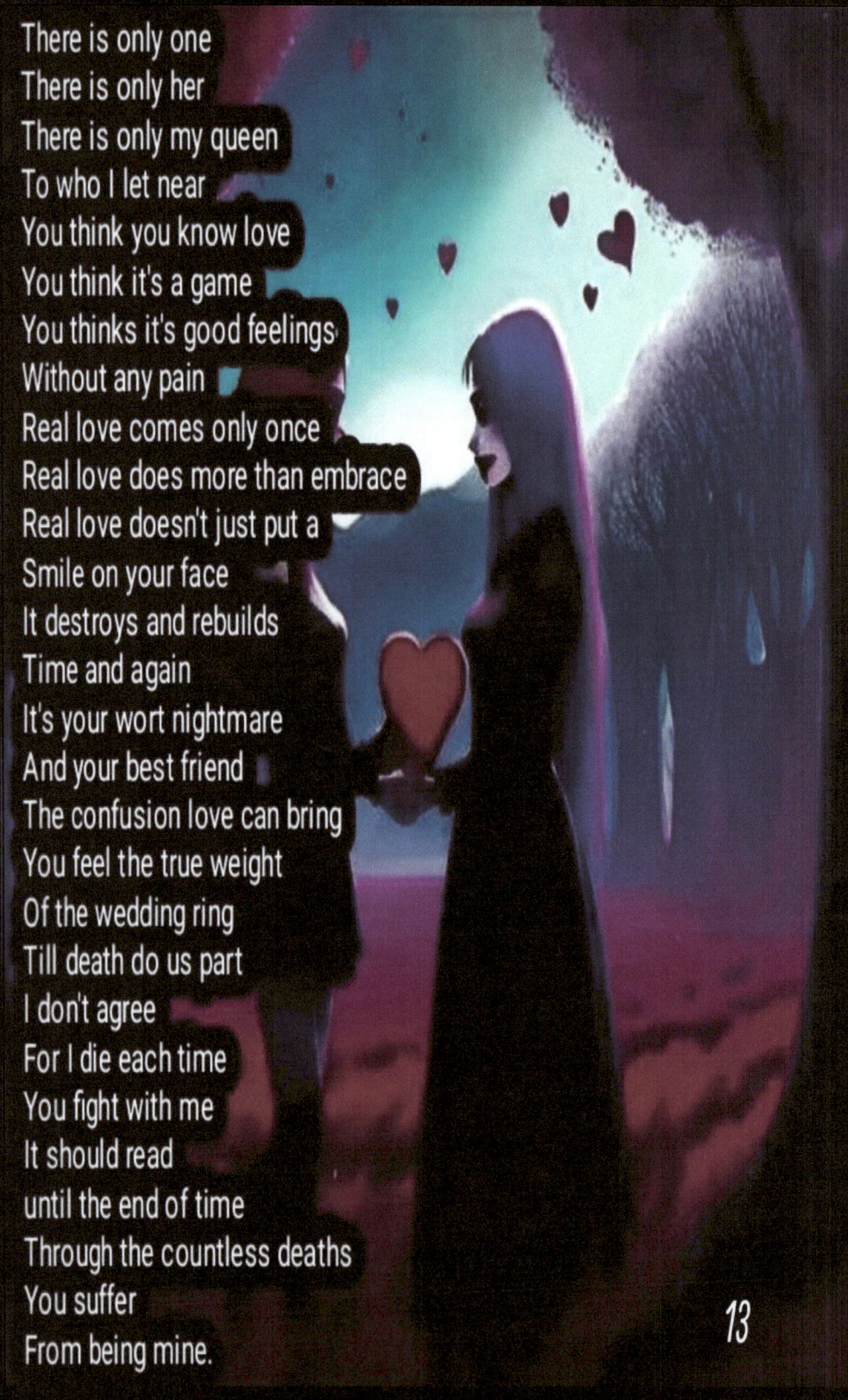

There is only one
There is only her
There is only my queen
To who I let near
You think you know love
You think it's a game
You thinks it's good feelings
Without any pain
Real love comes only once
Real love does more than embrace
Real love doesn't just put a
Smile on your face
It destroys and rebuilds
Time and again
It's your wort nightmare
And your best friend
The confusion love can bring
You feel the true weight
Of the wedding ring
Till death do us part
I don't agree
For I die each time
You fight with me
It should read
until the end of time
Through the countless deaths
You suffer
From being mine.

13

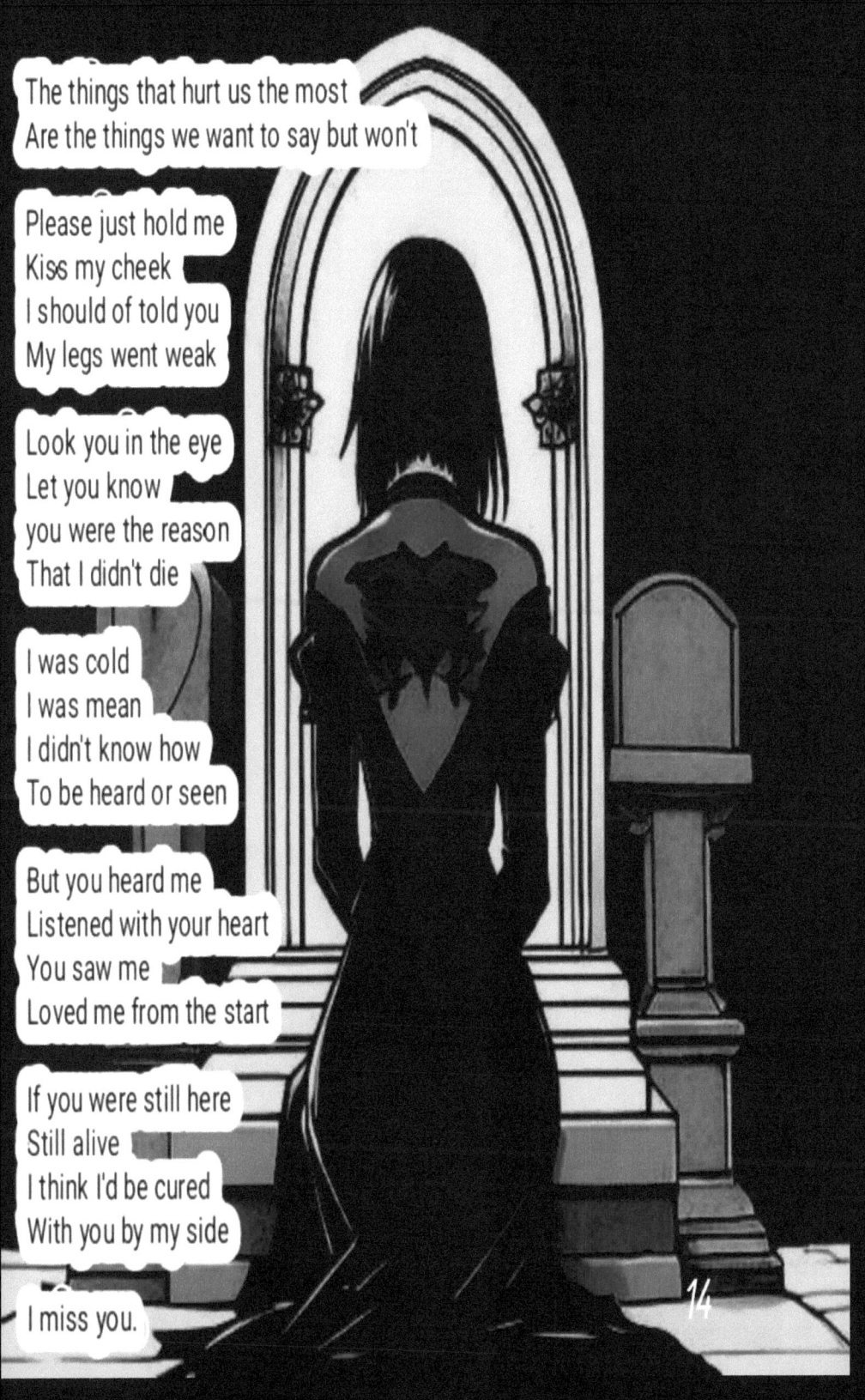

Social experiment
Leave the house
How long will I last
Away from control

Untested experience
How will I react
Try to see people
But all I see are threats

Mask the fear
It's all in your head

Deep breath
Focus
It won't hurt
It's good for you
Go for a walk
Better still
A brew and a talk

I'm here
It's OK their a friend
I'm safe

Enjoy the company
It was hard fought
Good to see you
how you doing
Fancy a night out
A drink, let loose

I know I can't do it
I still panic say yes

Where the fuck were you
You'd said you would come
That's the last fucking time
I invite you for fun

It's always the same
Untiil no friends are left
Leaving me Utterly And completely Bereft

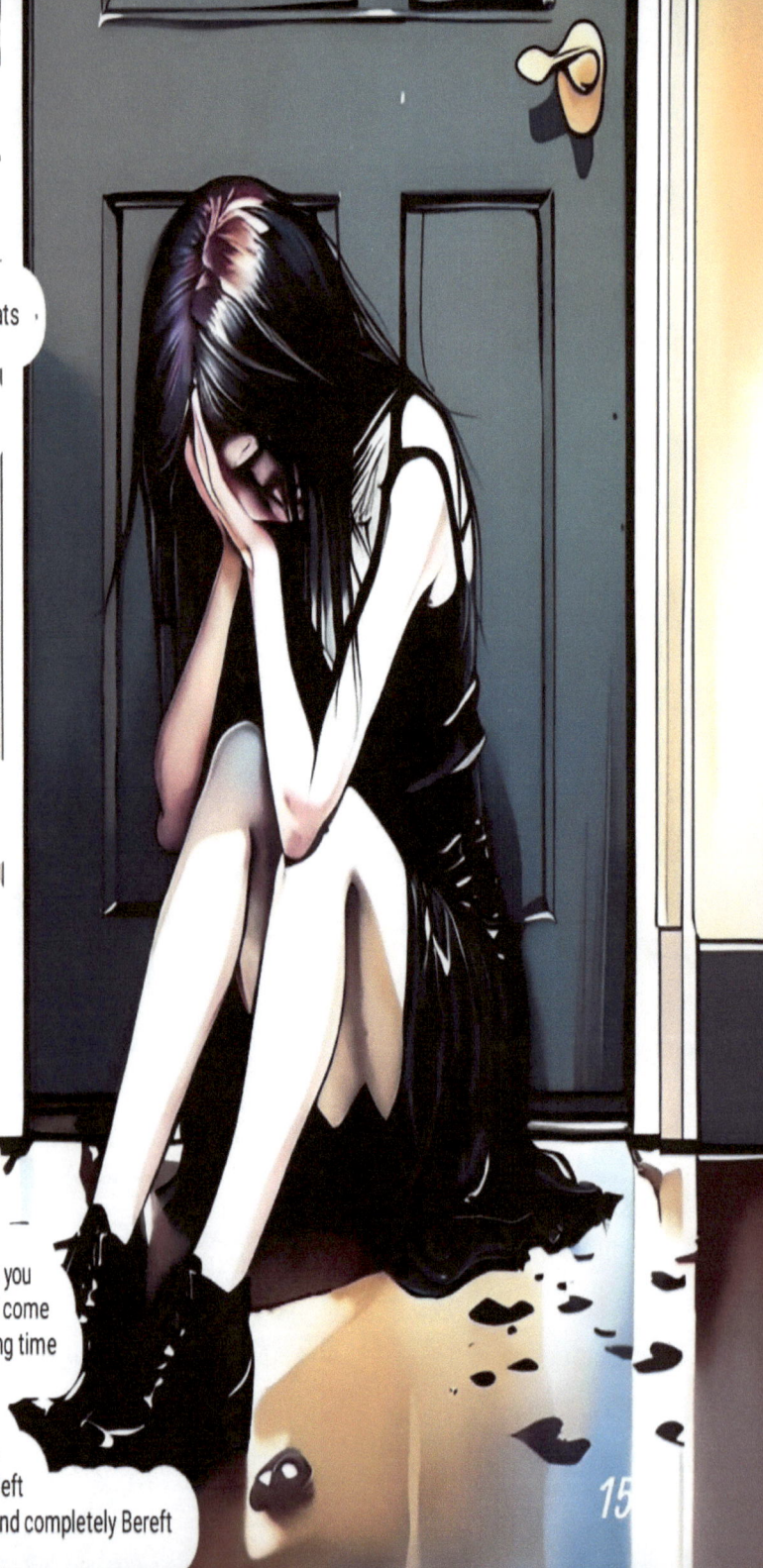

15

Wake up
Time for work
Whats the point
Minimum wage

Another day
Another pound
Feel like I'm working to the sound
Of digging my own grave in the ground

End of the month
Let's see the pay
Fuck
only enough to survive the day

Best get a loan
Create more debt
They want you to work until your dead
They hold the trigger against our heads

16

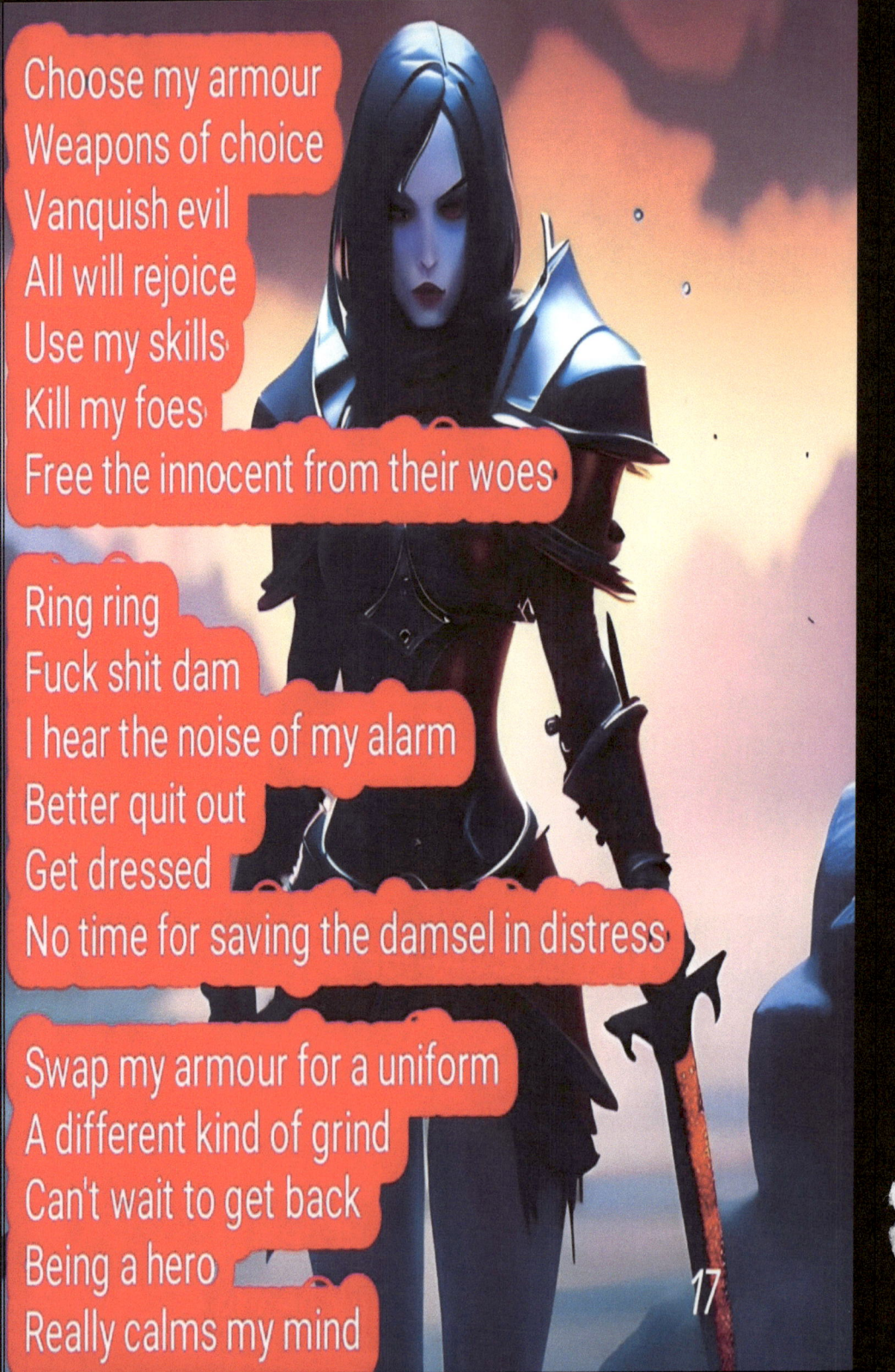

Choose my armour
Weapons of choice
Vanquish evil
All will rejoice
Use my skills
Kill my foes
Free the innocent from their woes

Ring ring
Fuck shit dam
I hear the noise of my alarm
Better quit out
Get dressed
No time for saving the damsel in distress

Swap my armour for a uniform
A different kind of grind
Can't wait to get back
Being a hero
Really calms my mind

17

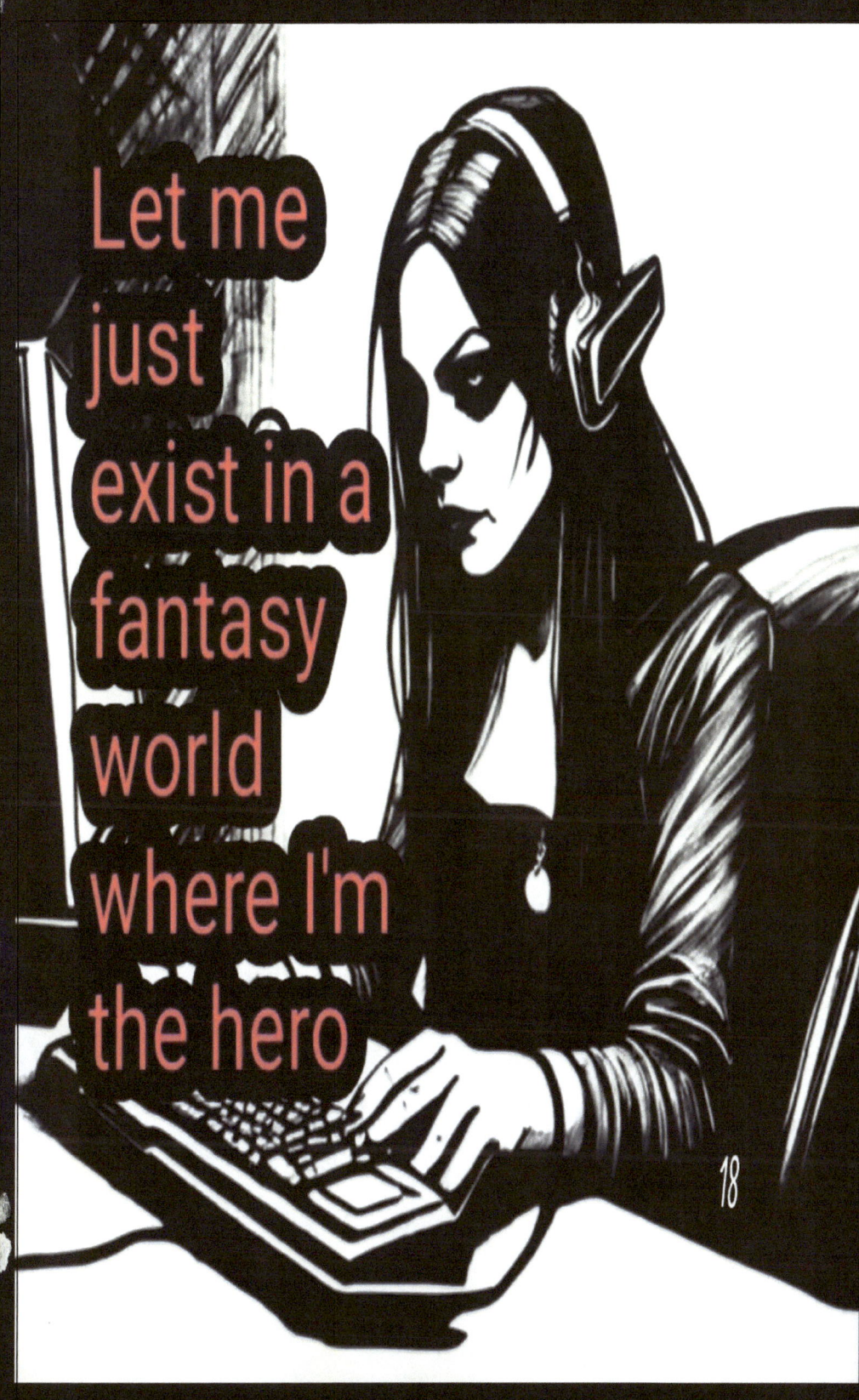

Apprehension
Unsettling fear
Orchestrated symphony of heartbeats
Muscles tense
Persistent unease
Reverberates through the body

Shadows cast on concentration
Sleep disturbed
Insinstent whispers
Sown seeds of irritability

Chronic anxiety
My constant companion
Springs from uncertainties
Therapeutic intervention
Prescribing me a peaceful day

19

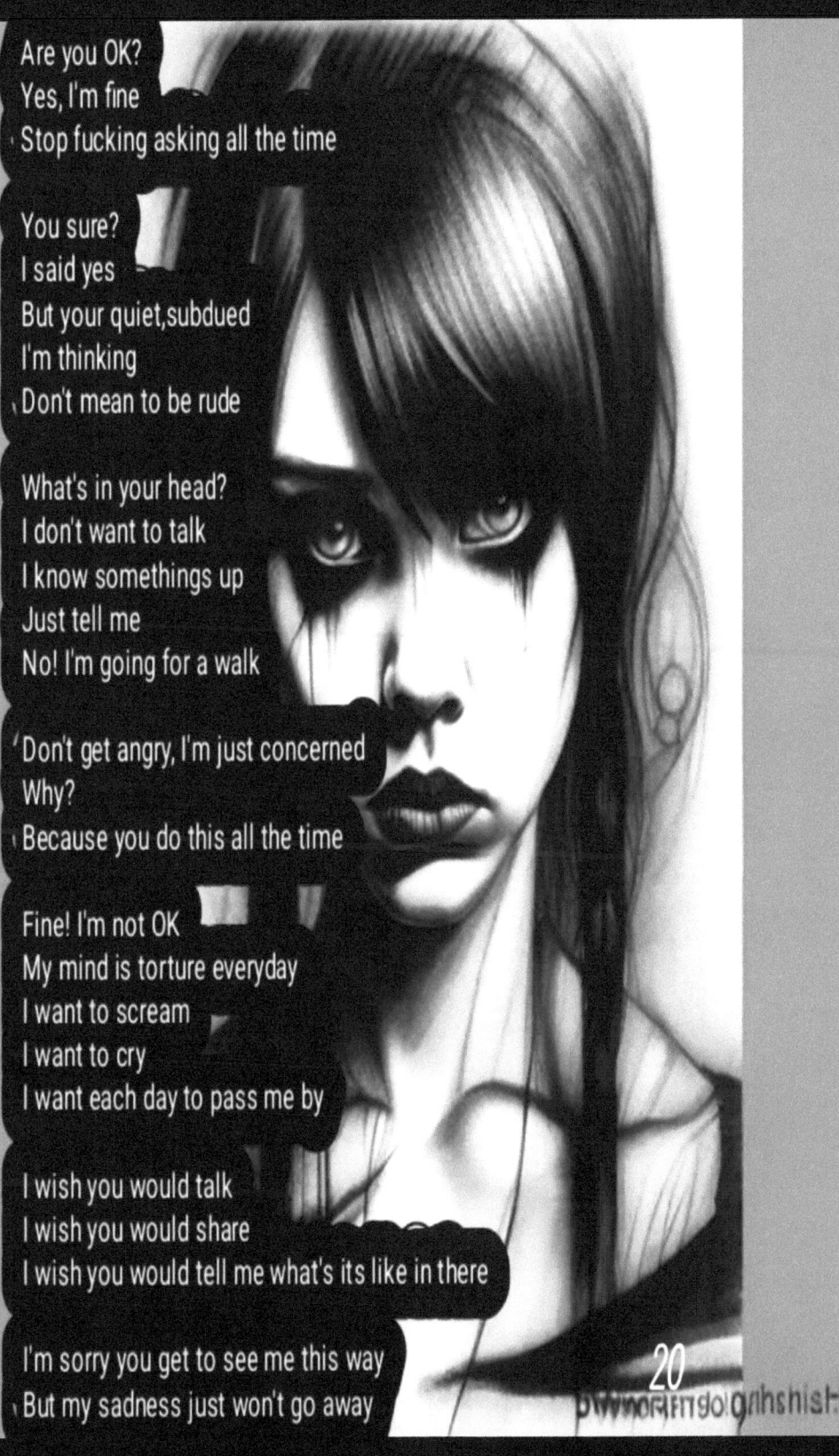

Are you OK?
Yes, I'm fine
Stop fucking asking all the time

You sure?
I said yes
But your quiet,subdued
I'm thinking
Don't mean to be rude

What's in your head?
I don't want to talk
I know somethings up
Just tell me
No! I'm going for a walk

Don't get angry, I'm just concerned
Why?
Because you do this all the time

Fine! I'm not OK
My mind is torture everyday
I want to scream
I want to cry
I want each day to pass me by

I wish you would talk
I wish you would share
I wish you would tell me what's its like in there

I'm sorry you get to see me this way
But my sadness just won't go away

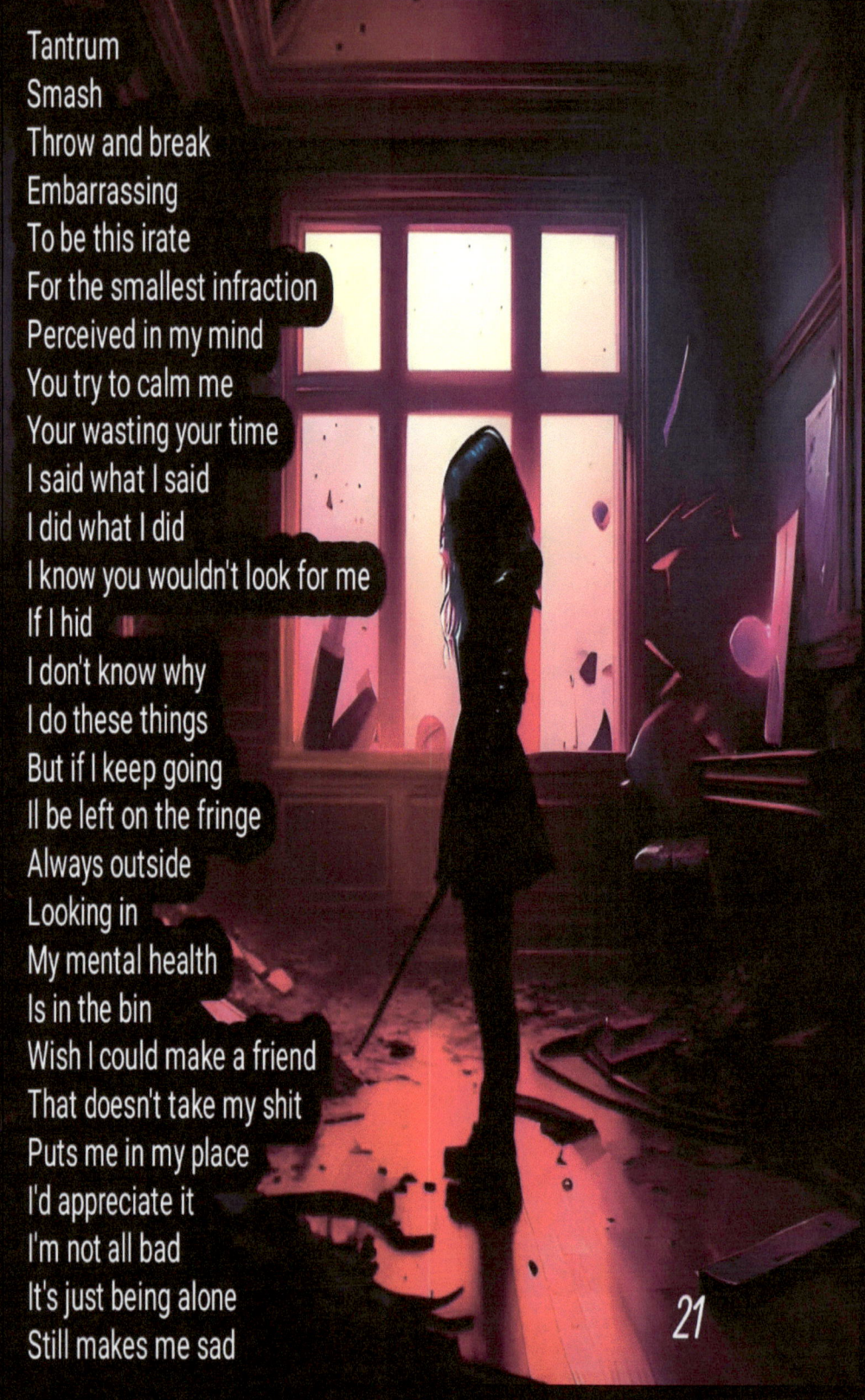

Tantrum
Smash
Throw and break
Embarrassing
To be this irate
For the smallest infraction
Perceived in my mind
You try to calm me
Your wasting your time
I said what I said
I did what I did
I know you wouldn't look for me
If I hid
I don't know why
I do these things
But if I keep going
Il be left on the fringe
Always outside
Looking in
My mental health
Is in the bin
Wish I could make a friend
That doesn't take my shit
Puts me in my place
I'd appreciate it
I'm not all bad
It's just being alone
Still makes me sad

21

A numbness cloaked in
skin's embrace,
comfort by touch, yet
vacant space

A paradox of tactile grace,
Sensation lost in time and
space

In the stillness of this
tactile trance
A paradoxical, hollow
romance.

For in the touch, no feeling
stirs, A paradox that
silently defers.

A brush of hands, a fleeting
caress
Yet the heart resides in
emptiness

22

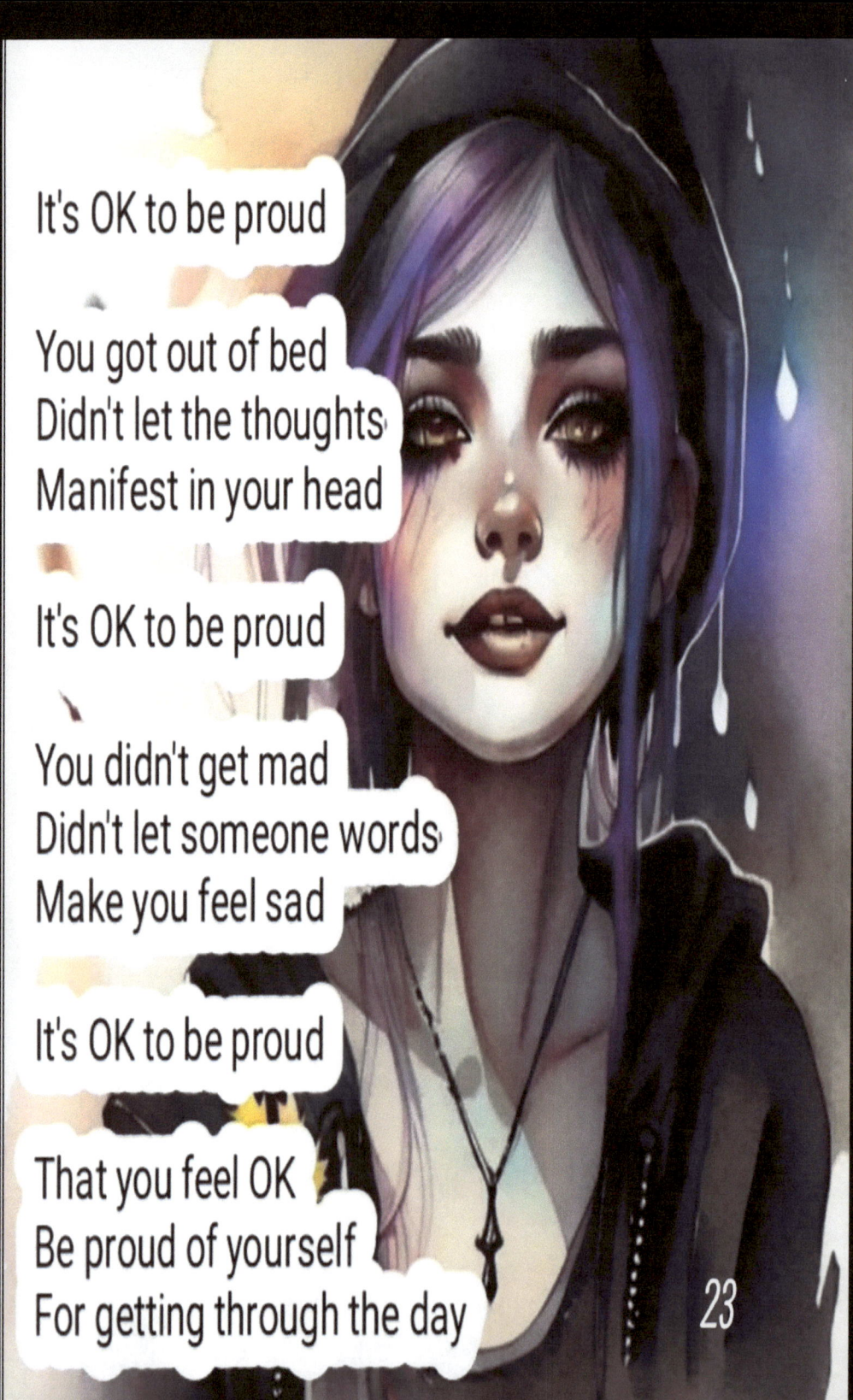

It's OK to be proud

You got out of bed
Didn't let the thoughts
Manifest in your head

It's OK to be proud

You didn't get mad
Didn't let someone words
Make you feel sad

It's OK to be proud

That you feel OK
Be proud of yourself
For getting through the day

23

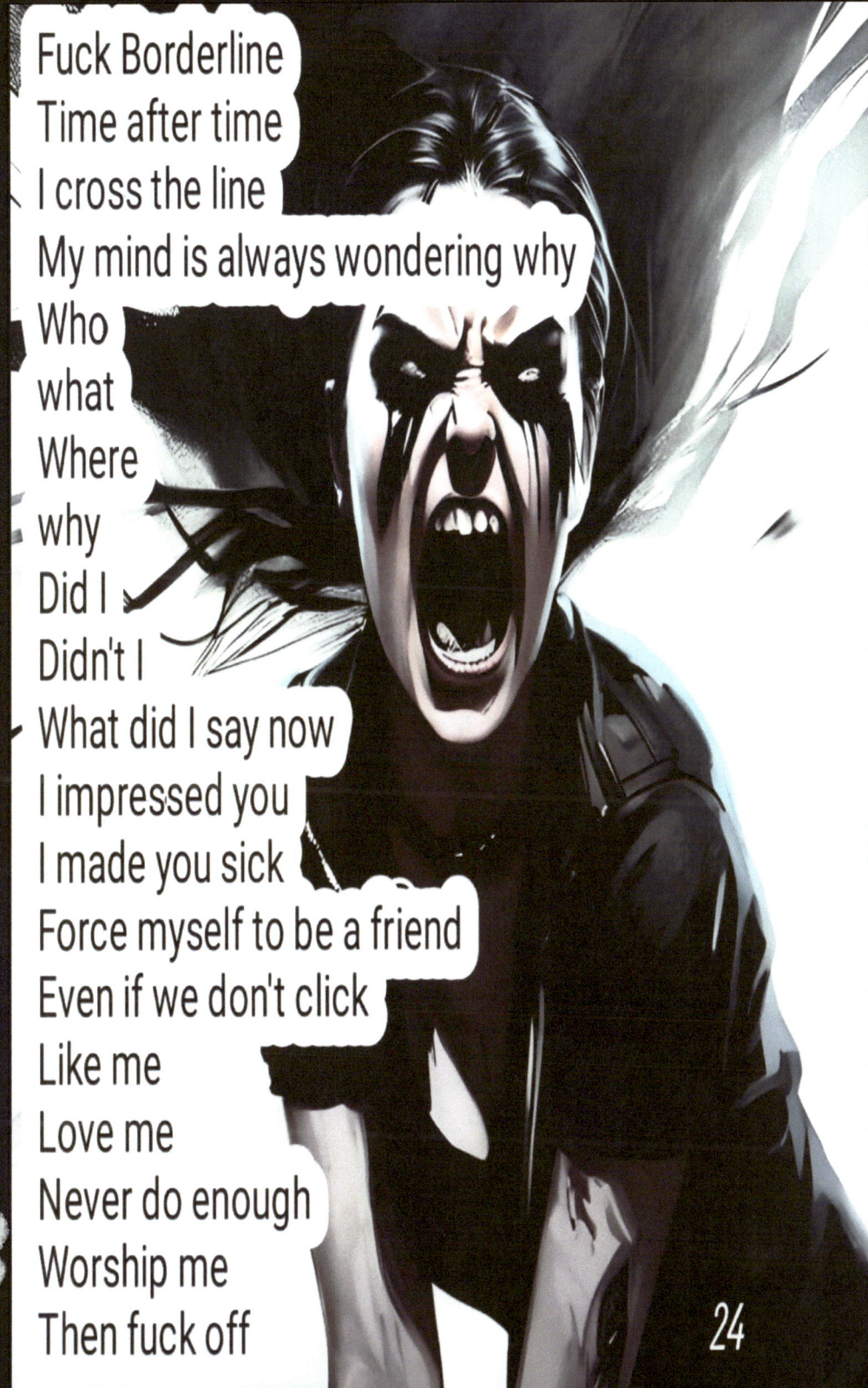

Fuck Borderline
Time after time
I cross the line
My mind is always wondering why
Who
what
Where
why
Did I
Didn't I
What did I say now
I impressed you
I made you sick
Force myself to be a friend
Even if we don't click
Like me
Love me
Never do enough
Worship me
Then fuck off

24

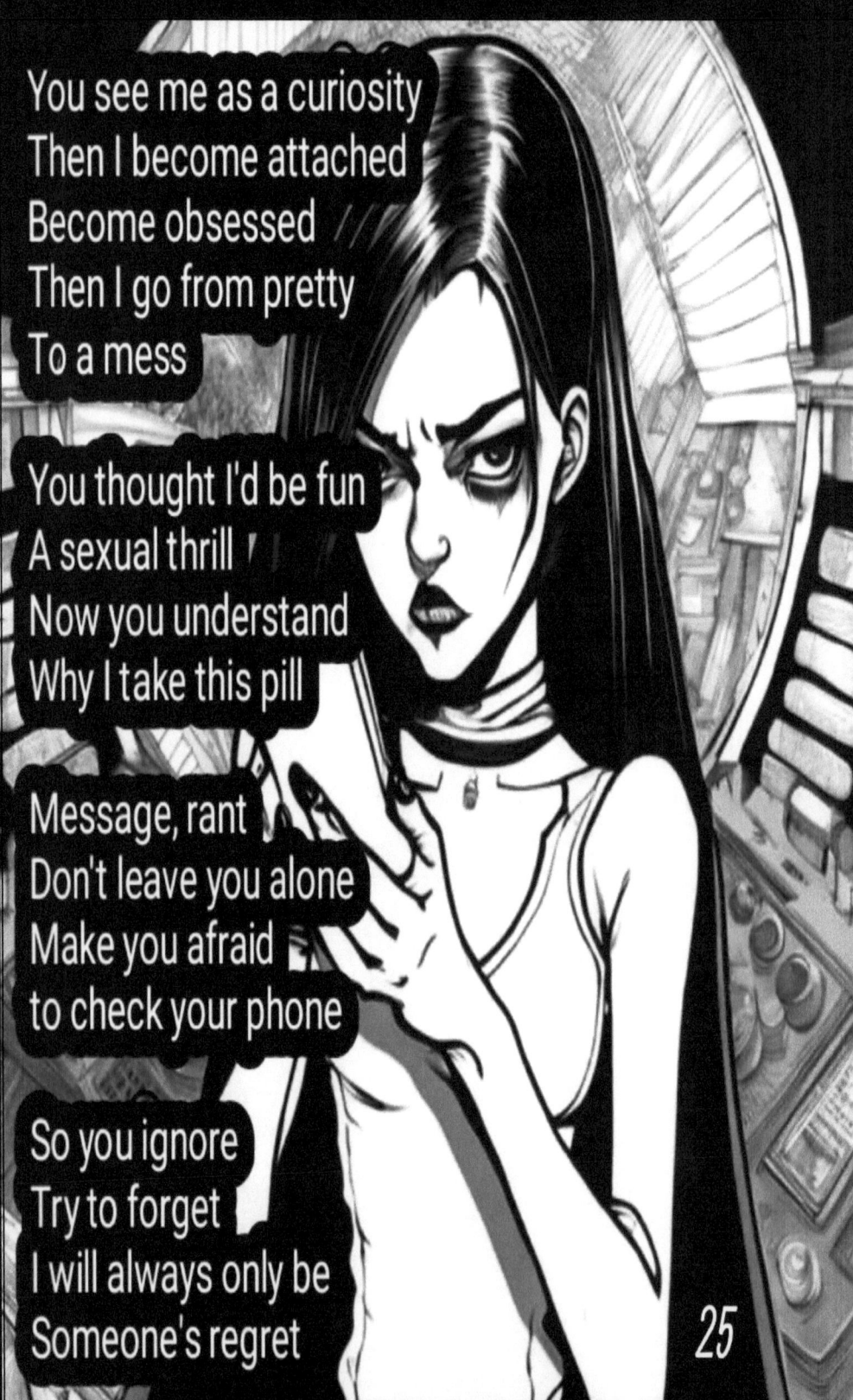

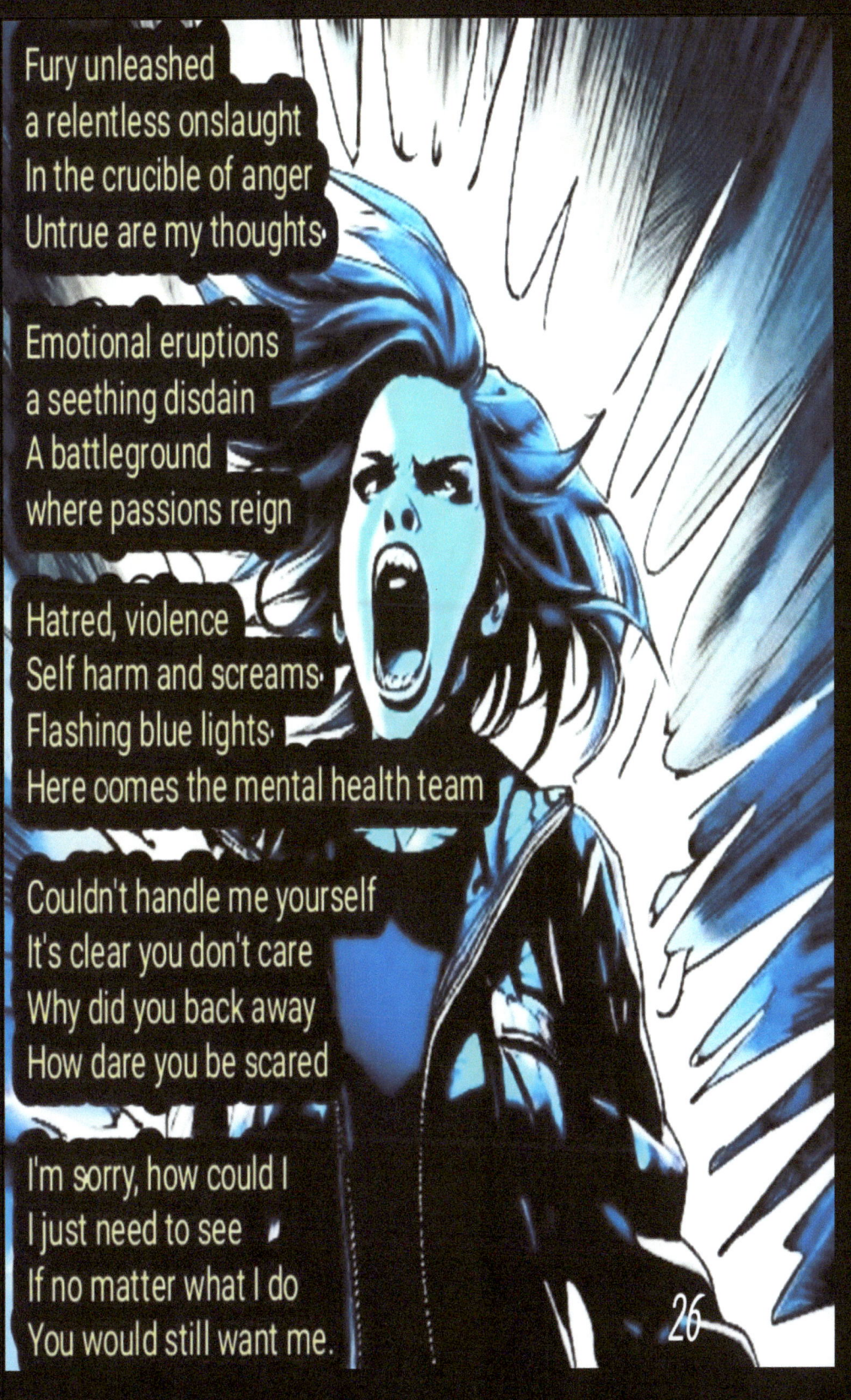

Fury unleashed
a relentless onslaught
In the crucible of anger
Untrue are my thoughts

Emotional eruptions
a seething disdain
A battleground
where passions reign

Hatred, violence
Self harm and screams
Flashing blue lights
Here comes the mental health team

Couldn't handle me yourself
It's clear you don't care
Why did you back away
How dare you be scared

I'm sorry, how could I
I just need to see
If no matter what I do
You would still want me.

26

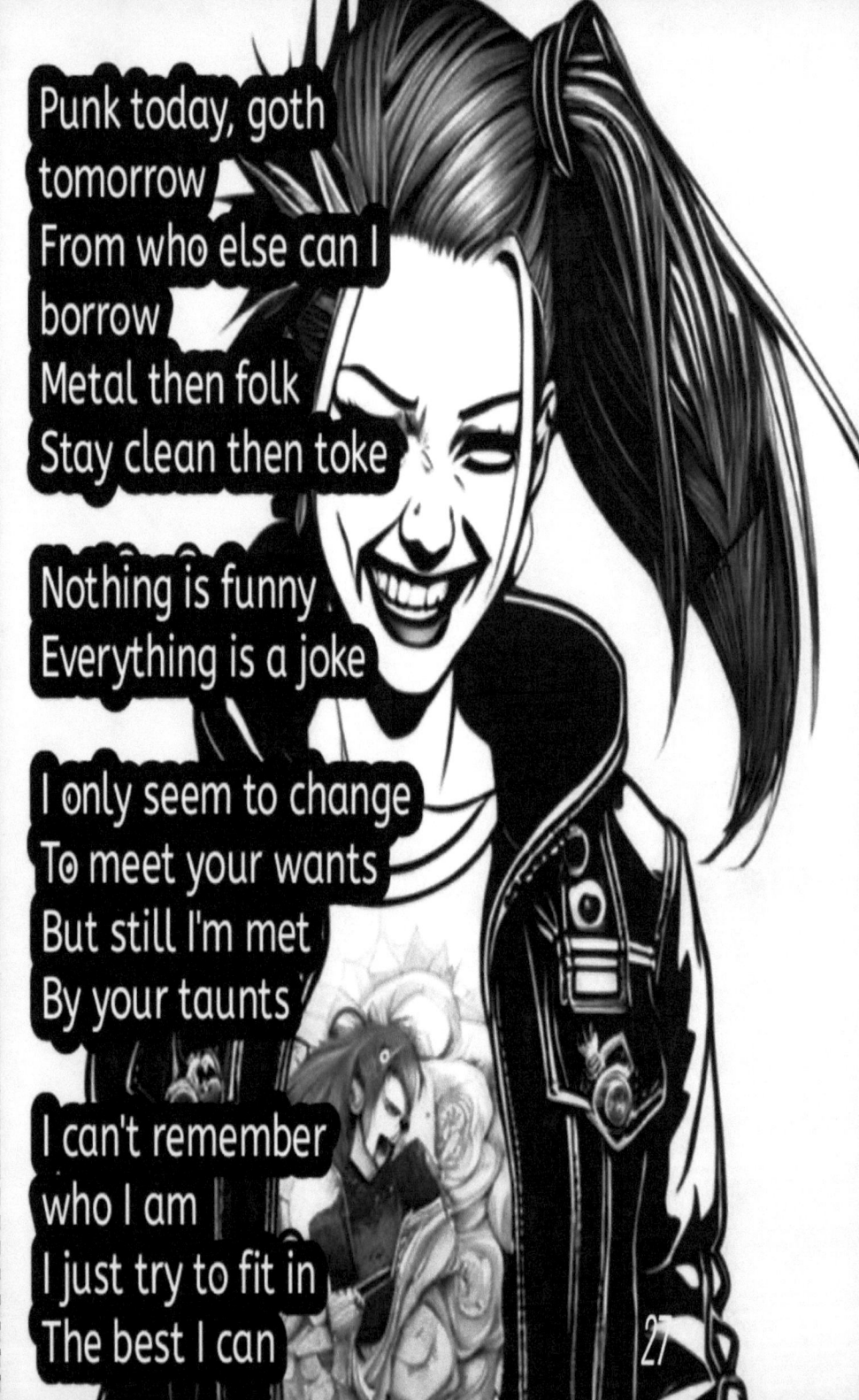

Punk today, goth
tomorrow
From who else can I
borrow
Metal then folk
Stay clean then toke

Nothing is funny
Everything is a joke

I only seem to change
To meet your wants
But still I'm met
By your taunts

I can't remember
who I am
I just try to fit in
The best I can

27

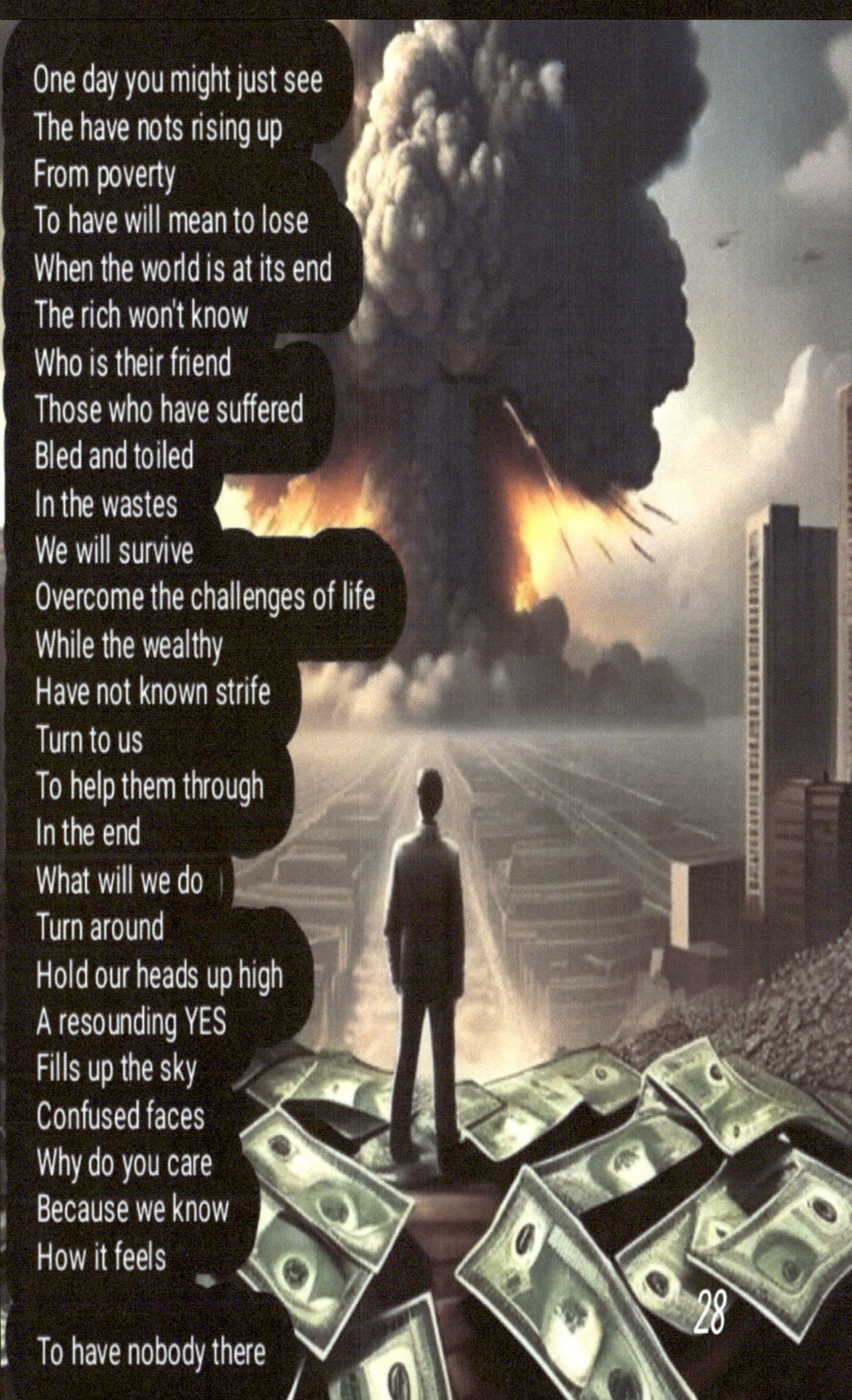

One day you might just see
The have nots rising up
From poverty
To have will mean to lose
When the world is at its end
The rich won't know
Who is their friend
Those who have suffered
Bled and toiled
In the wastes
We will survive
Overcome the challenges of life
While the wealthy
Have not known strife
Turn to us
To help them through
In the end
What will we do
Turn around
Hold our heads up high
A resounding YES
Fills up the sky
Confused faces
Why do you care
Because we know
How it feels

To have nobody there

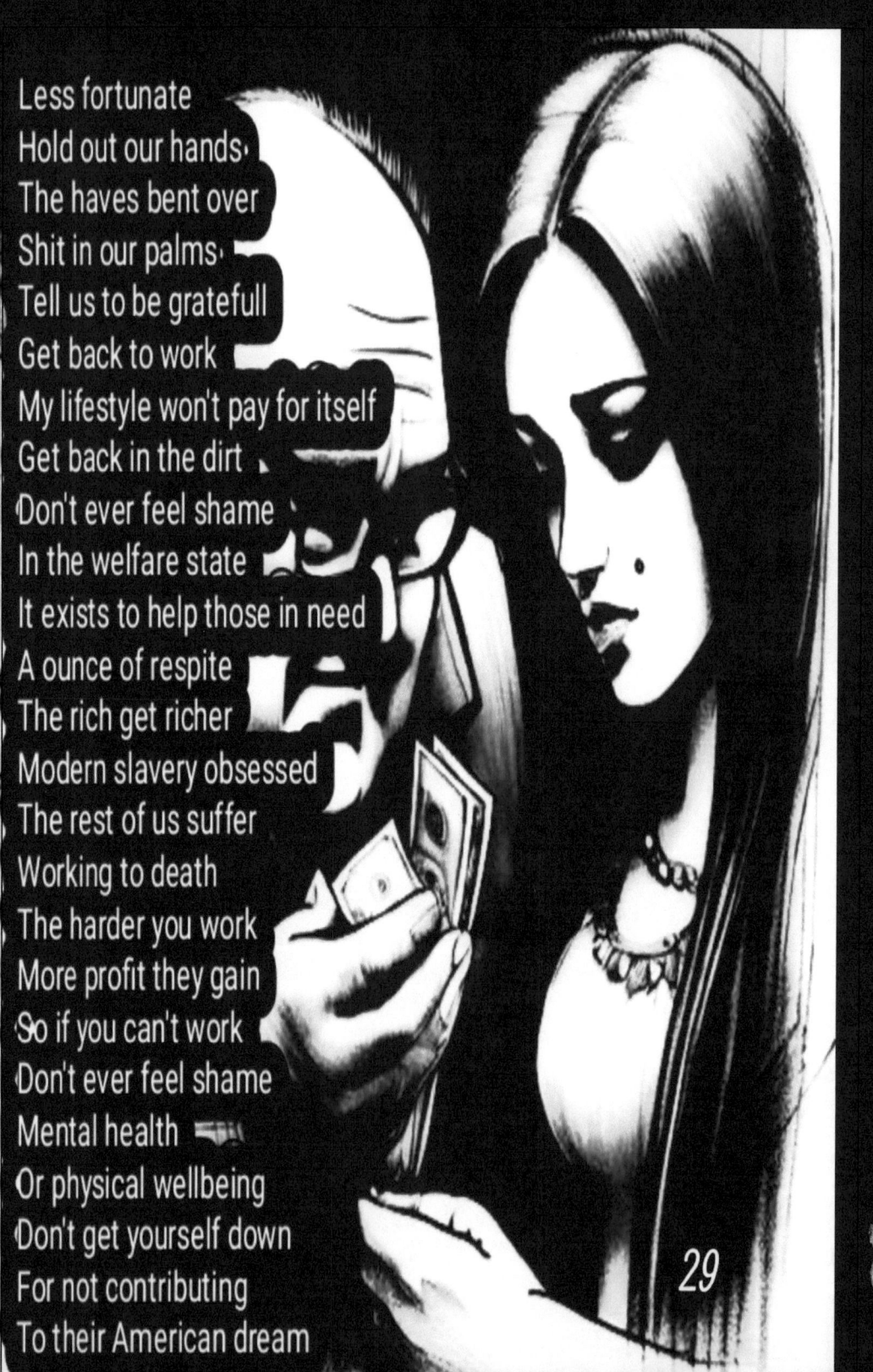

Less fortunate
Hold out our hands
The haves bent over
Shit in our palms
Tell us to be gratefull
Get back to work
My lifestyle won't pay for itself
Get back in the dirt
Don't ever feel shame
In the welfare state
It exists to help those in need
A ounce of respite
The rich get richer
Modern slavery obsessed
The rest of us suffer
Working to death
The harder you work
More profit they gain
So if you can't work
Don't ever feel shame
Mental health
Or physical wellbeing
Don't get yourself down
For not contributing
To their American dream

29

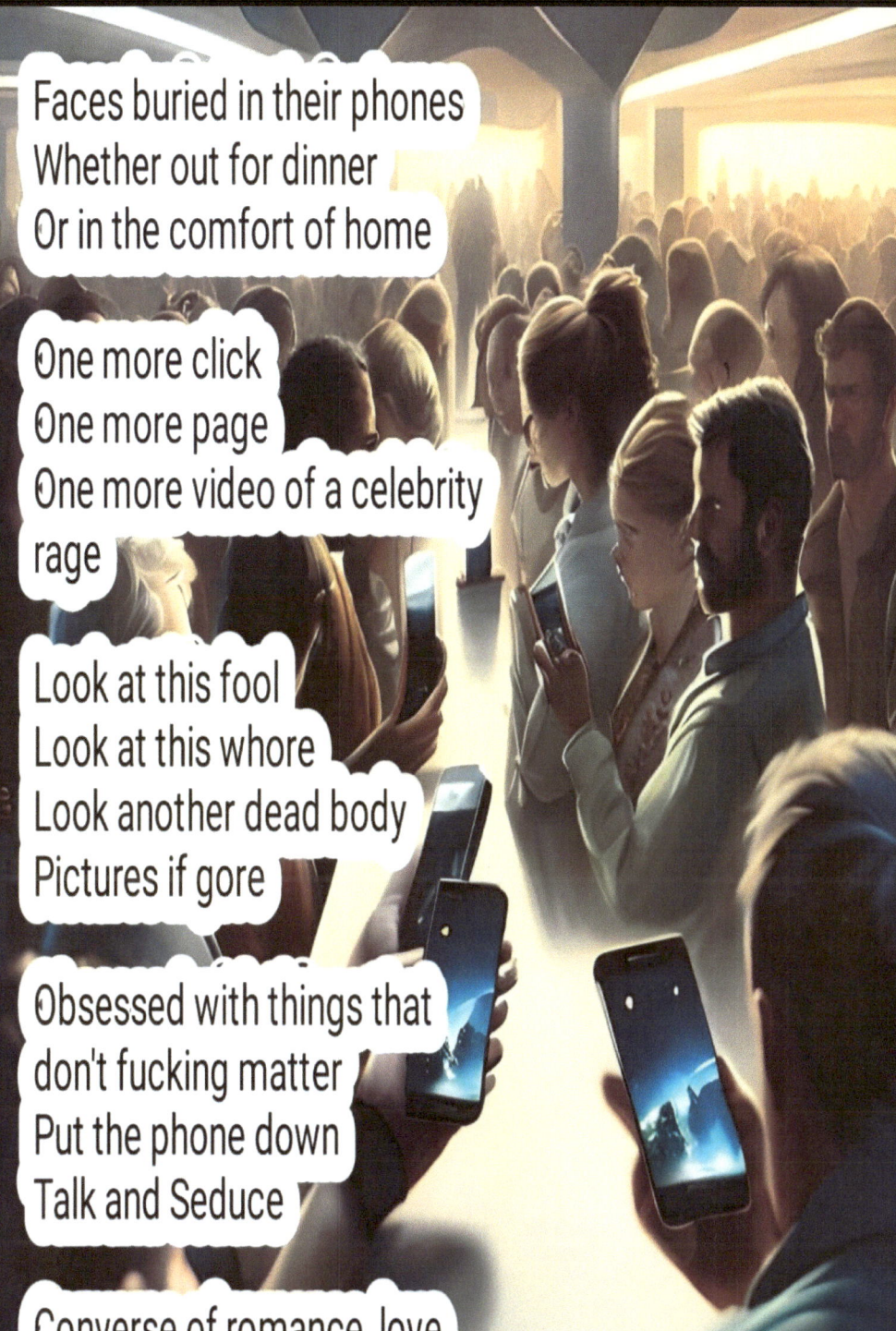

Faces buried in their phones
Whether out for dinner
Or in the comfort of home

One more click
One more page
One more video of a celebrity
rage

Look at this fool
Look at this whore
Look another dead body
Pictures if gore

Obsessed with things that
don't fucking matter
Put the phone down
Talk and Seduce

Converse of romance, love
and truth

30

I created the cage you
live in
only I can set you free.
To do that I must
destroy myself.
If I give you the tools,
will you do it for me

31

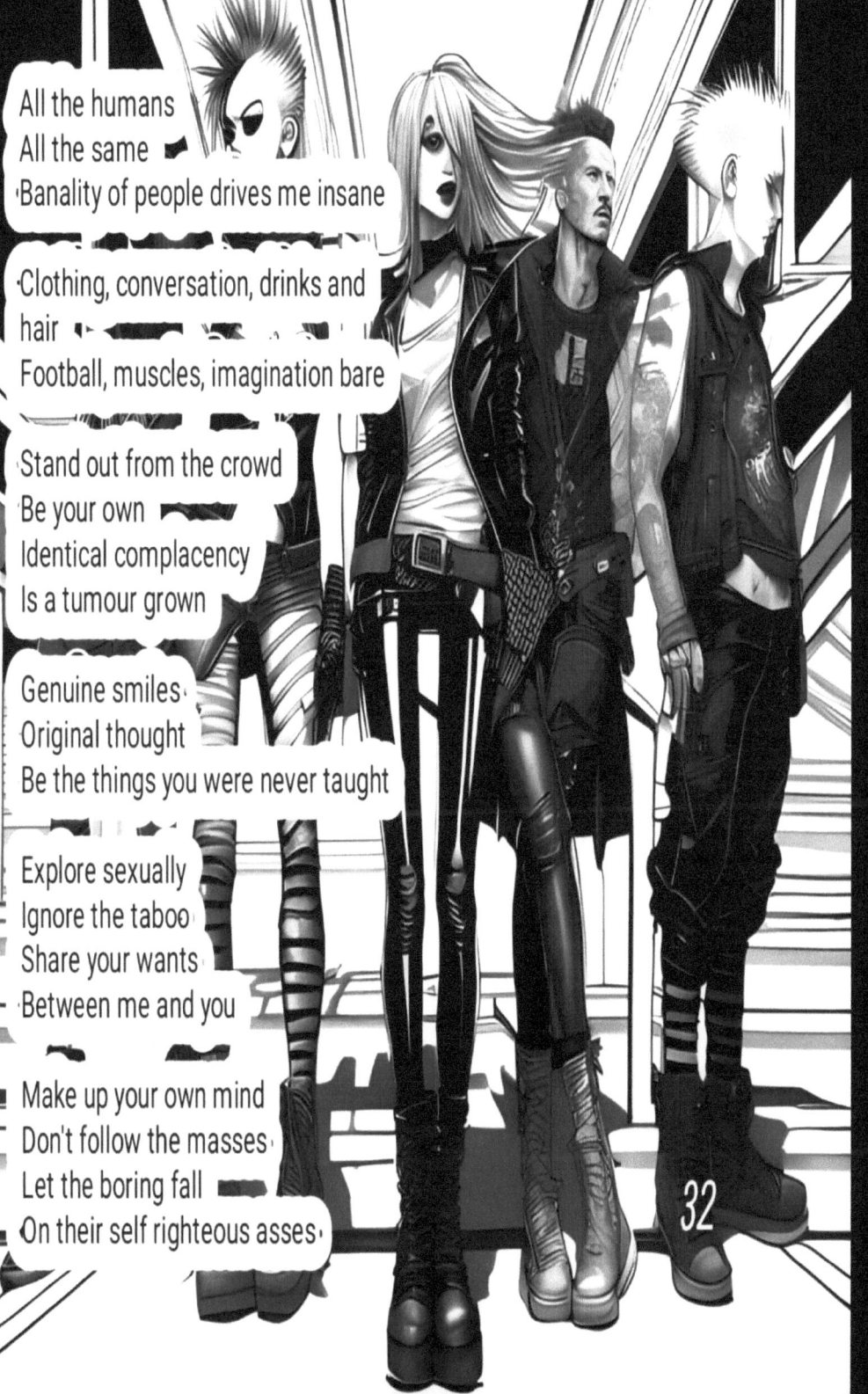

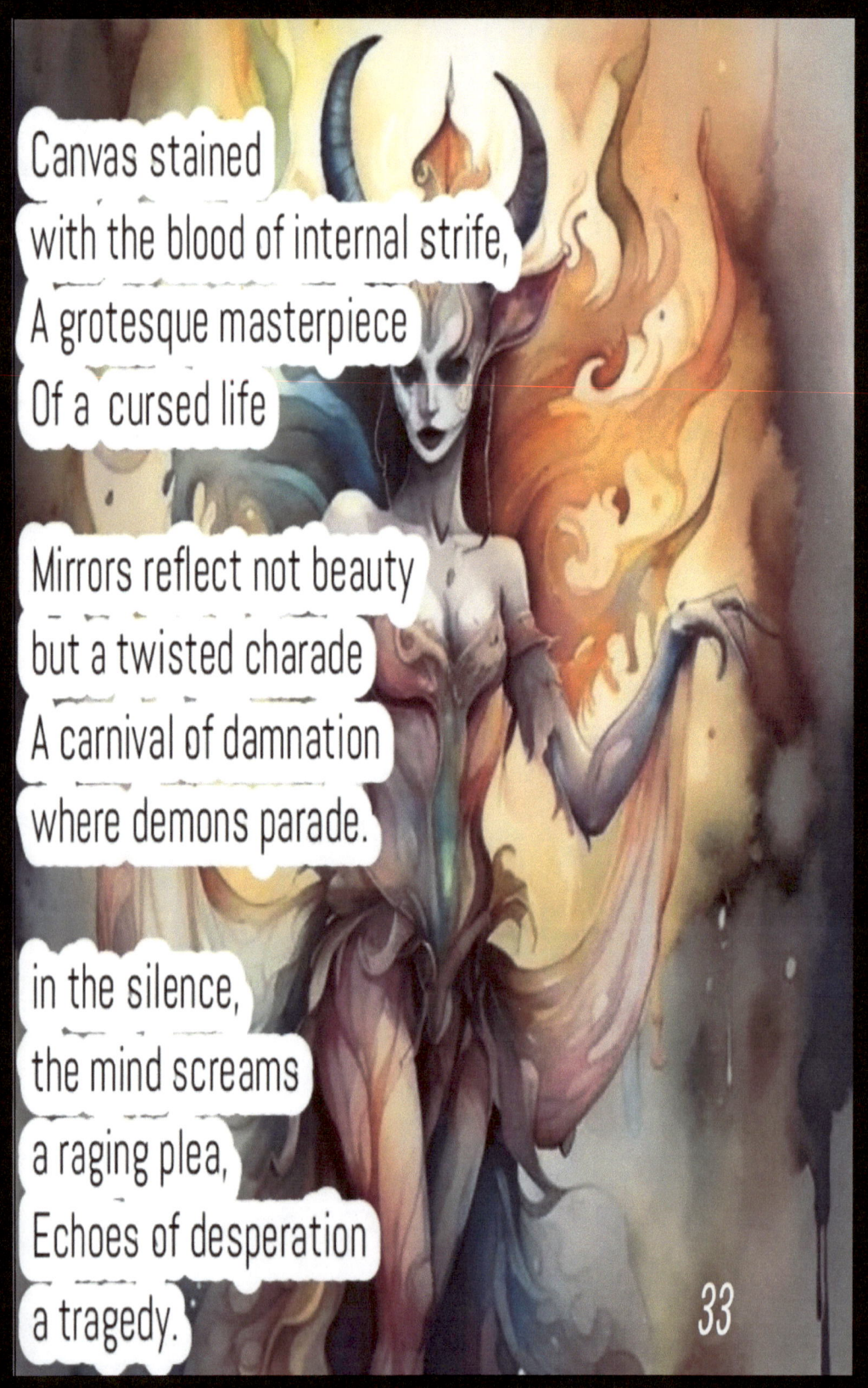

Canvas stained
with the blood of internal strife,
A grotesque masterpiece
Of a cursed life

Mirrors reflect not beauty
but a twisted charade
A carnival of damnation
where demons parade.

in the silence,
the mind screams
a raging plea,
Echoes of desperation
a tragedy.

33

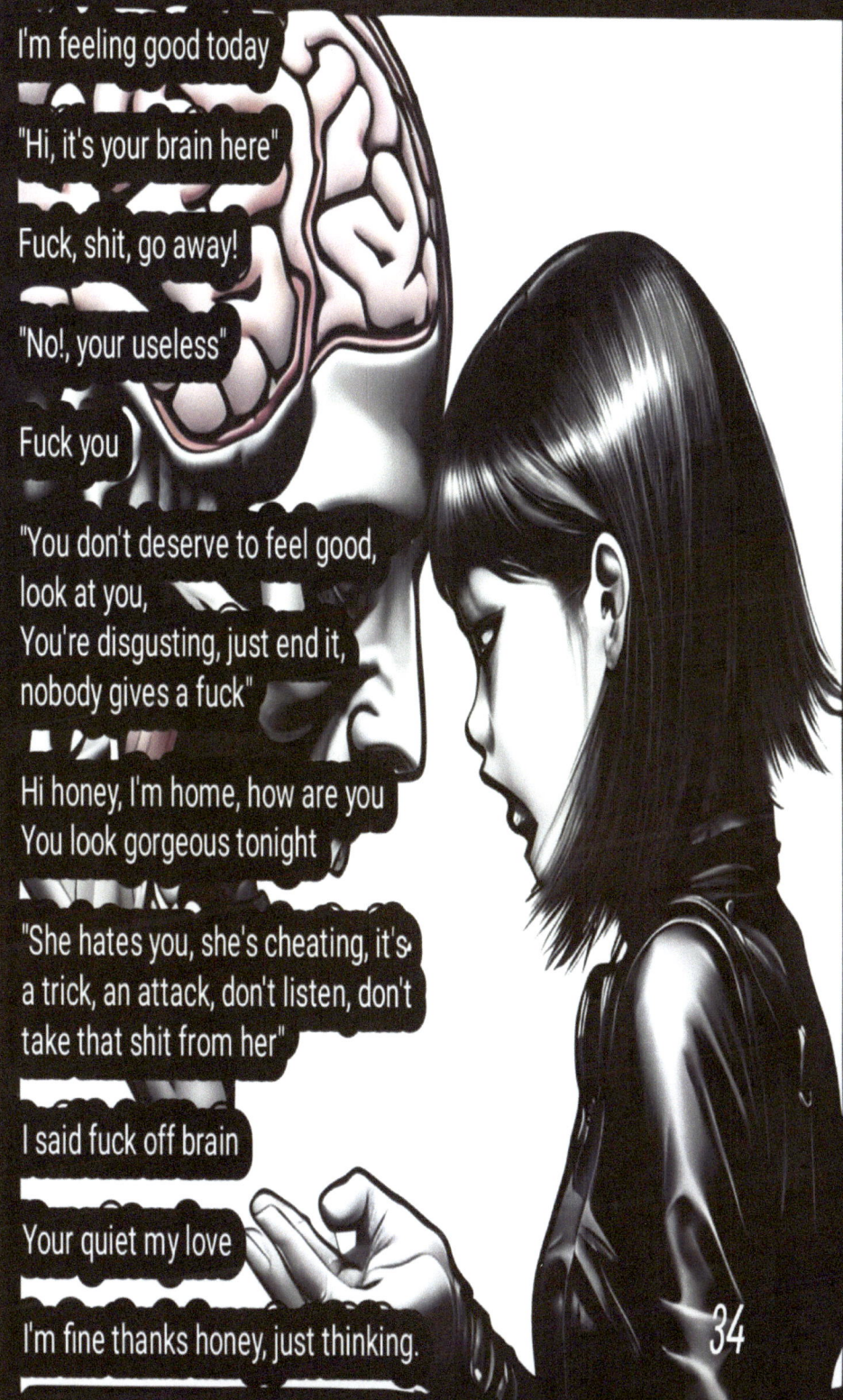

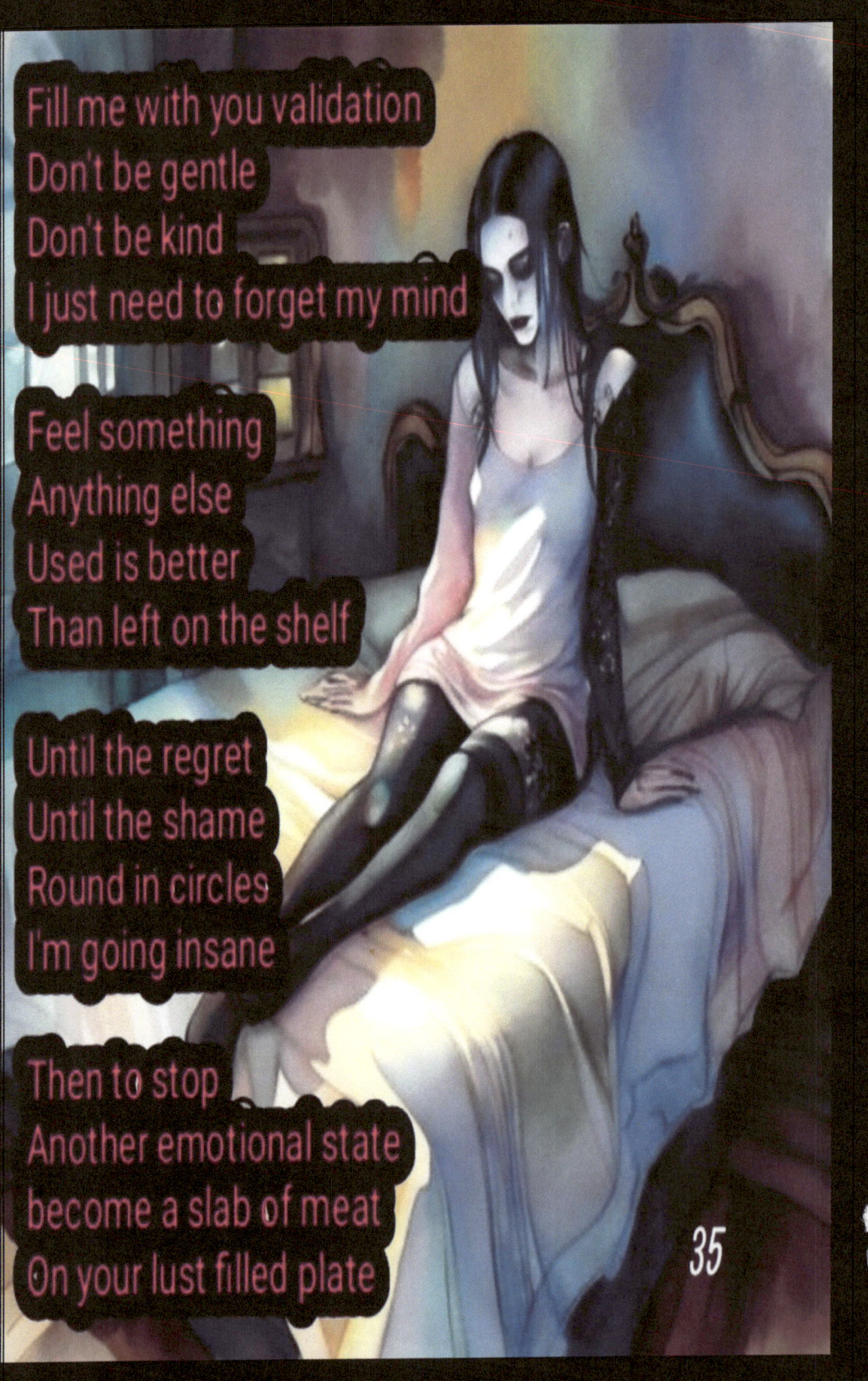

Fill me with you validation
Don't be gentle
Don't be kind
I just need to forget my mind

Feel something
Anything else
Used is better
Than left on the shelf

Until the regret
Until the shame
Round in circles
I'm going insane

Then to stop
Another emotional state
become a slab of meat
On your lust filled plate

35

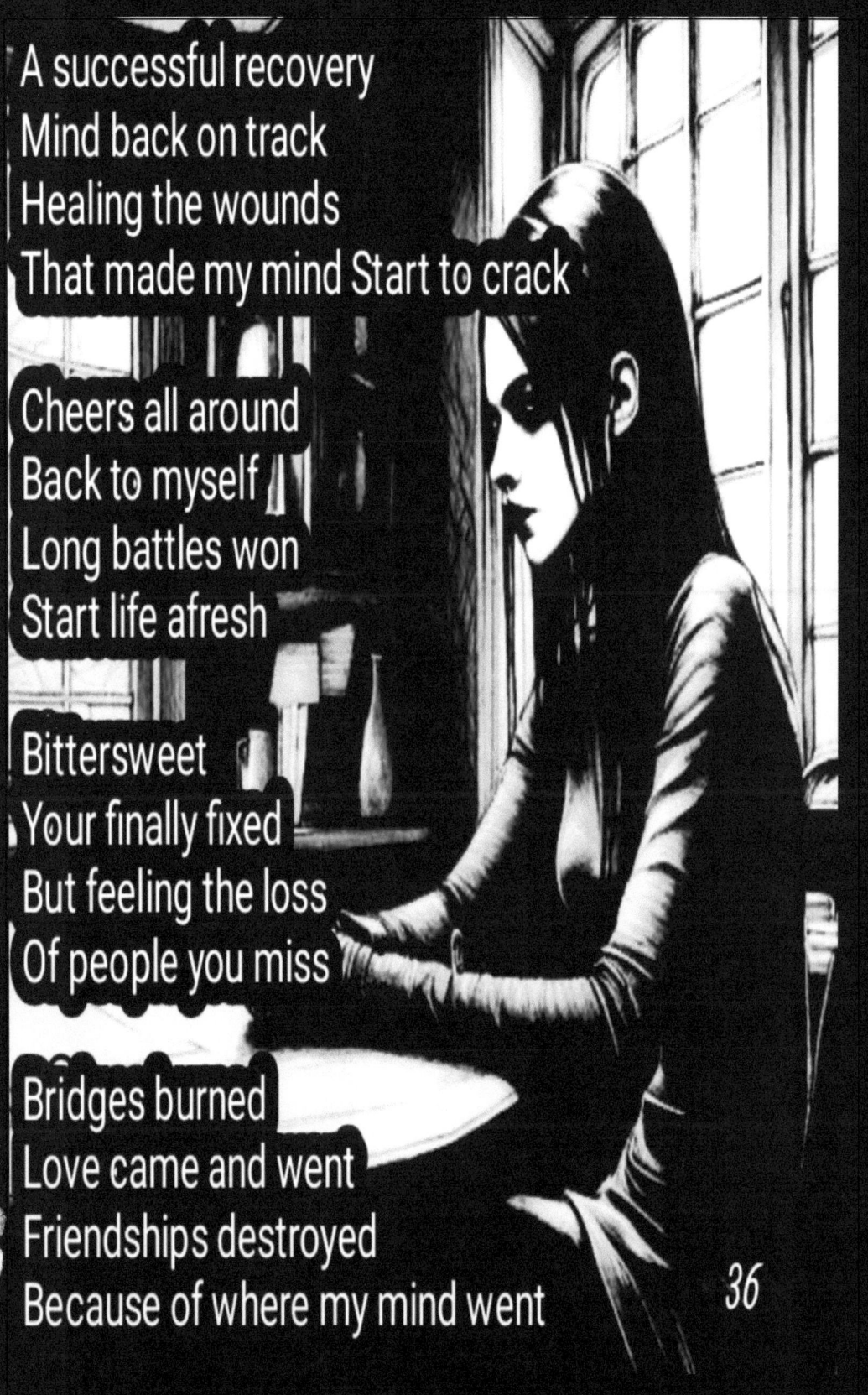

A successful recovery
Mind back on track
Healing the wounds
That made my mind Start to crack

Cheers all around
Back to myself
Long battles won
Start life afresh

Bittersweet
Your finally fixed
But feeling the loss
Of people you miss

Bridges burned
Love came and went
Friendships destroyed
Because of where my mind went

36

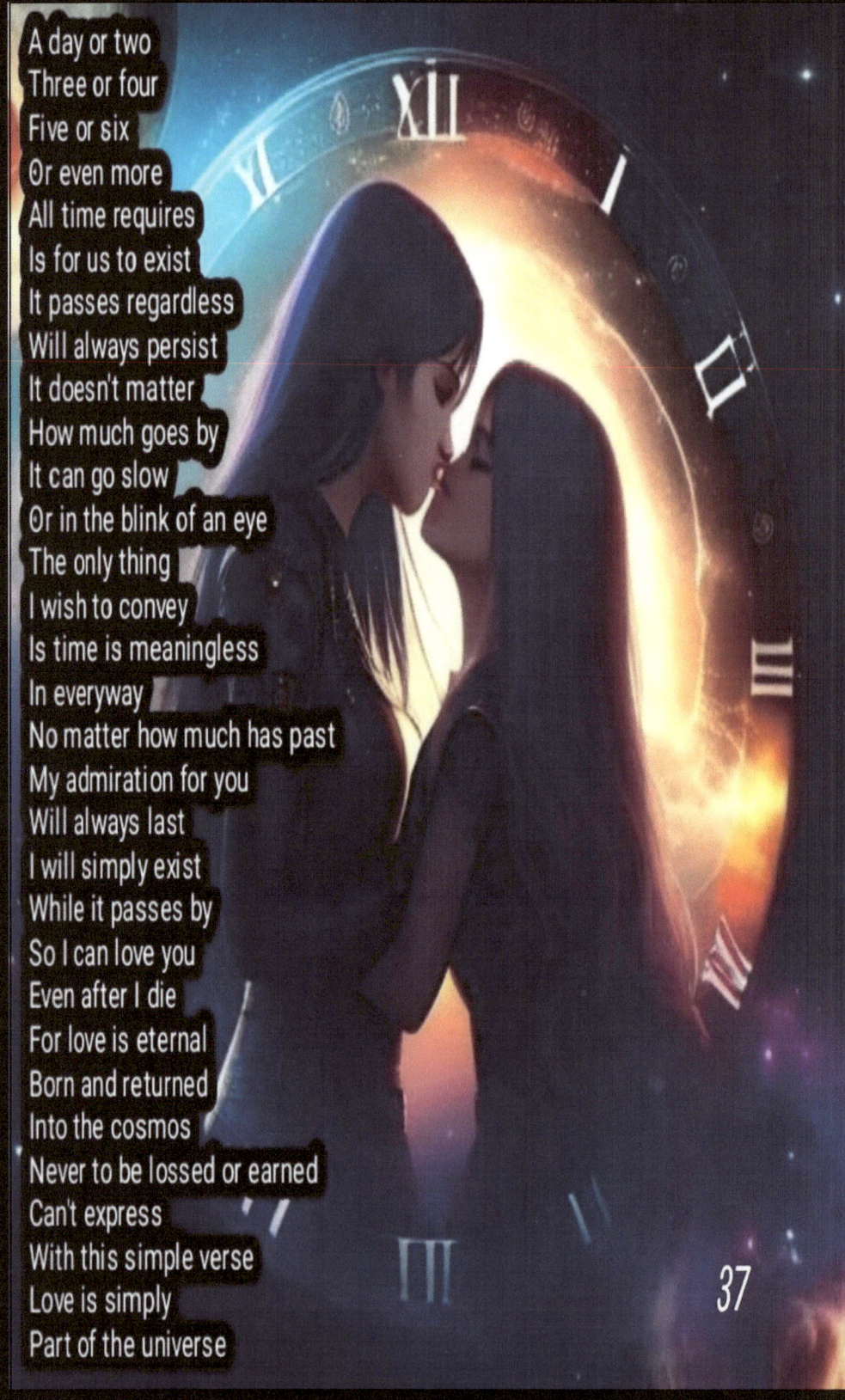

A day or two
Three or four
Five or six
Or even more
All time requires
Is for us to exist
It passes regardless
Will always persist
It doesn't matter
How much goes by
It can go slow
Or in the blink of an eye
The only thing
I wish to convey
Is time is meaningless
In everyway
No matter how much has past
My admiration for you
Will always last
I will simply exist
While it passes by
So I can love you
Even after I die
For love is eternal
Born and returned
Into the cosmos
Never to be lossed or earned
Can't express
With this simple verse
Love is simply
Part of the universe

37

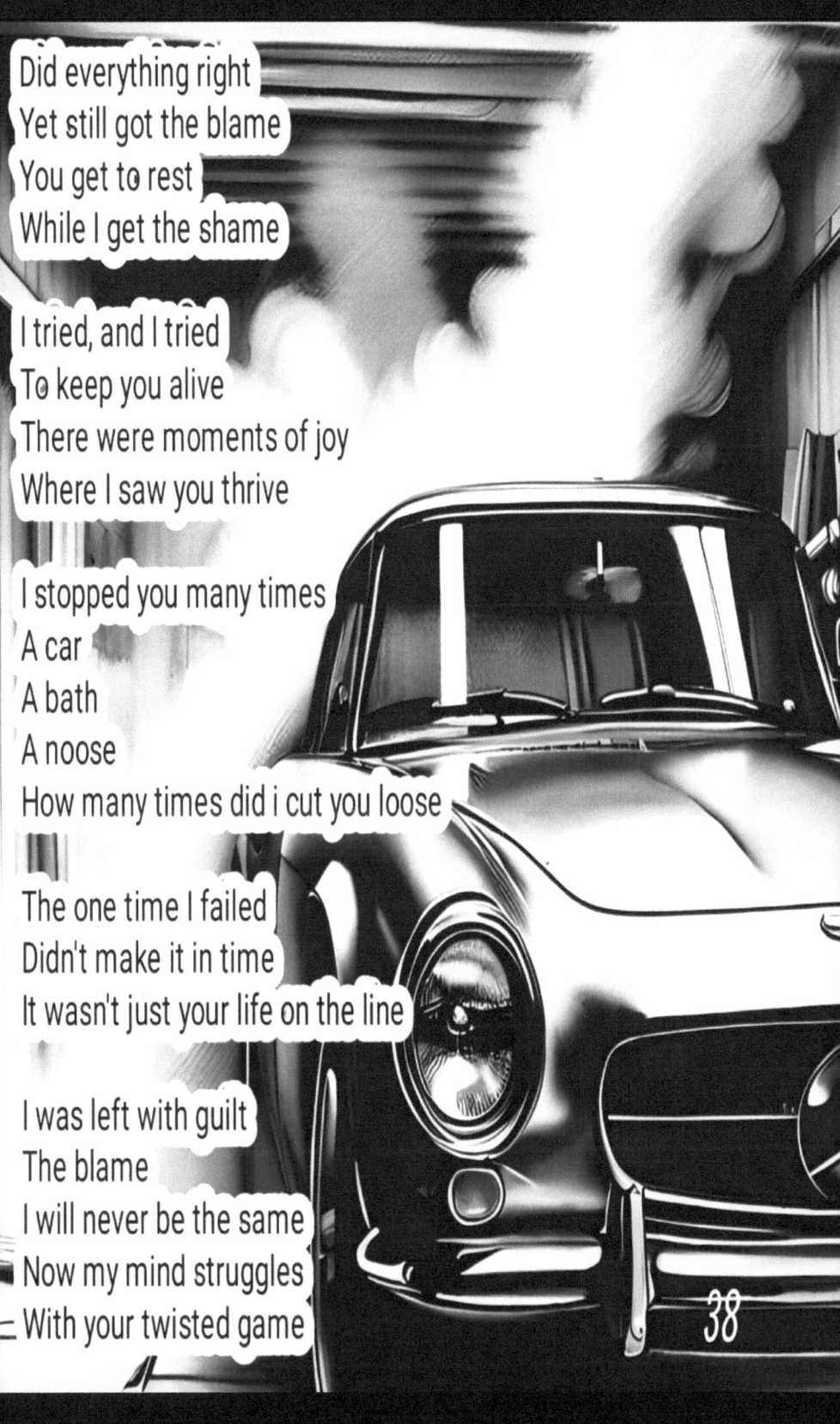

Did everything right
Yet still got the blame
You get to rest
While I get the shame

I tried, and I tried
To keep you alive
There were moments of joy
Where I saw you thrive

I stopped you many times
A car
A bath
A noose
How many times did i cut you loose

The one time I failed
Didn't make it in time
It wasn't just your life on the line

I was left with guilt
The blame
I will never be the same
Now my mind struggles
With your twisted game

38

Can you hear me
now I'm silent
The words of myths and lies
Spoken as truth
Can you hear me
Or just the swinging of the noose
Can you hear me
When my anger has stopped
Can you hear me
Now I'm no longer blaming you
Can you hear me
Even though you never listened
Can you hear me
Or do you refuse, out of sight now
Out of mind
Or do you hear how you left me behind
Can you hear me
My voice, my pain
Or is the silence a relief
No longer burdened by my beliefs
Can you hear me
Is there silence and peace
Do you still think what could of been
If I didn't end up unheard and unseen

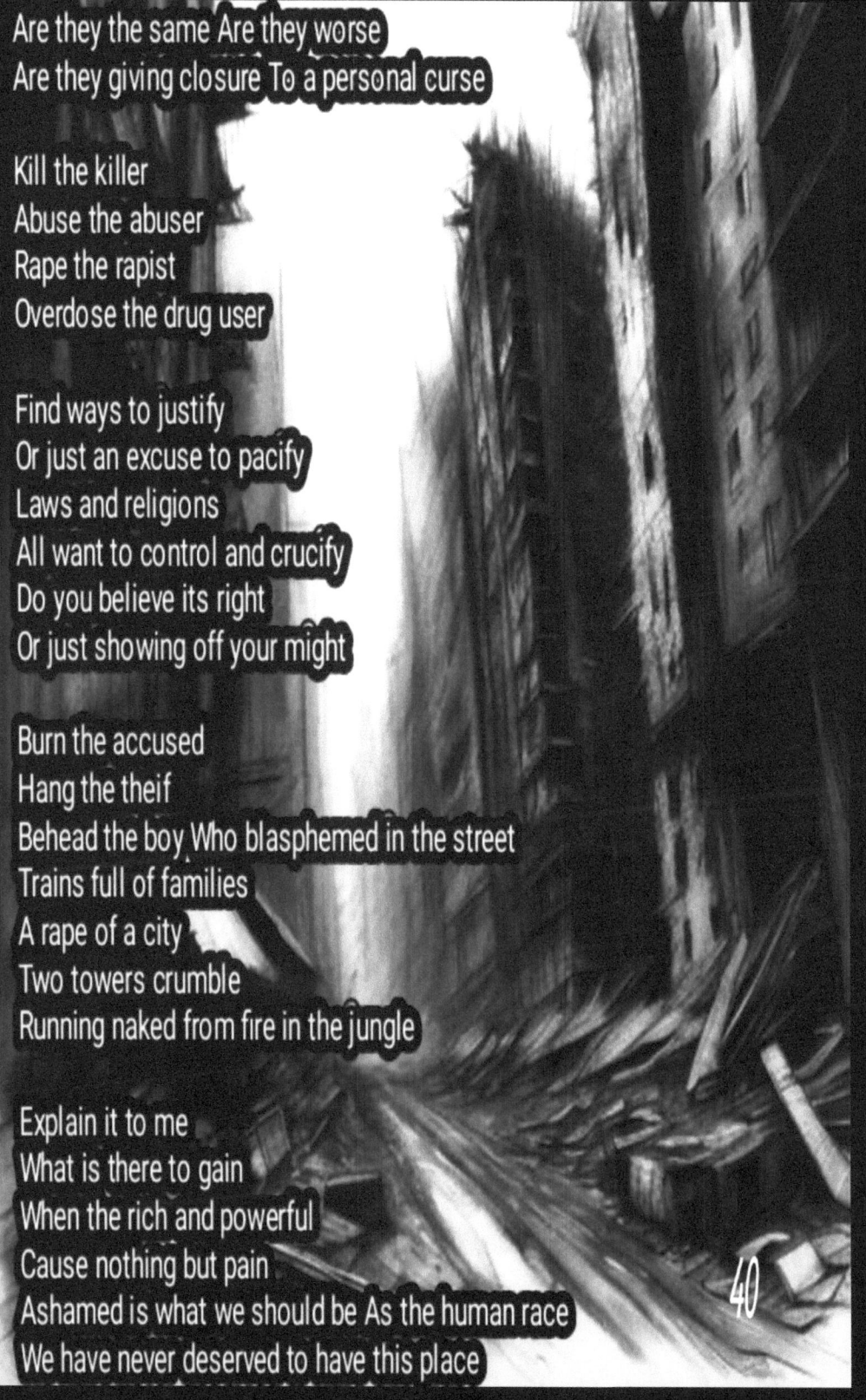

Are they the same Are they worse
Are they giving closure To a personal curse

Kill the killer
Abuse the abuser
Rape the rapist
Overdose the drug user

Find ways to justify
Or just an excuse to pacify
Laws and religions
All want to control and crucify
Do you believe its right
Or just showing off your might

Burn the accused
Hang the theif
Behead the boy Who blasphemed in the street
Trains full of families
A rape of a city
Two towers crumble
Running naked from fire in the jungle

Explain it to me
What is there to gain
When the rich and powerful
Cause nothing but pain
Ashamed is what we should be As the human race
We have never deserved to have this place

40

YOUR NOT WRONG FOR FEELING SAD

THE WORLD DOESN'T NEED TO UNDERSTAND

41

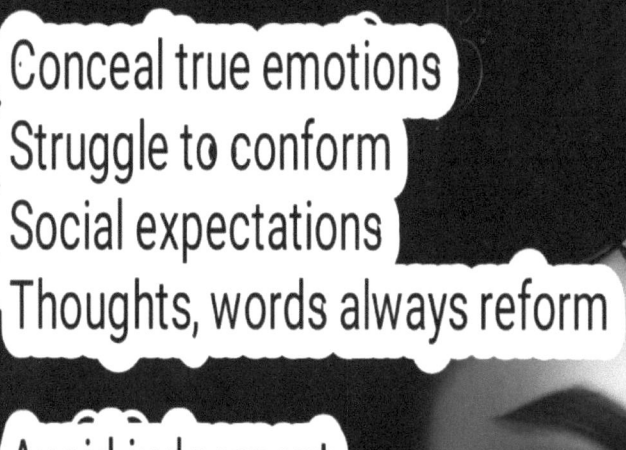

Conceal true emotions
Struggle to conform
Social expectations
Thoughts, words always reform

Avoid judgement
Navigate the social
Suppression of the genuine
Make my action's allign

Navigate challenges
But contributes to stress
Hinders my ability
To emotionally express

Disconnection
From ones true self
Cloak my struggles
Mental stealth

42

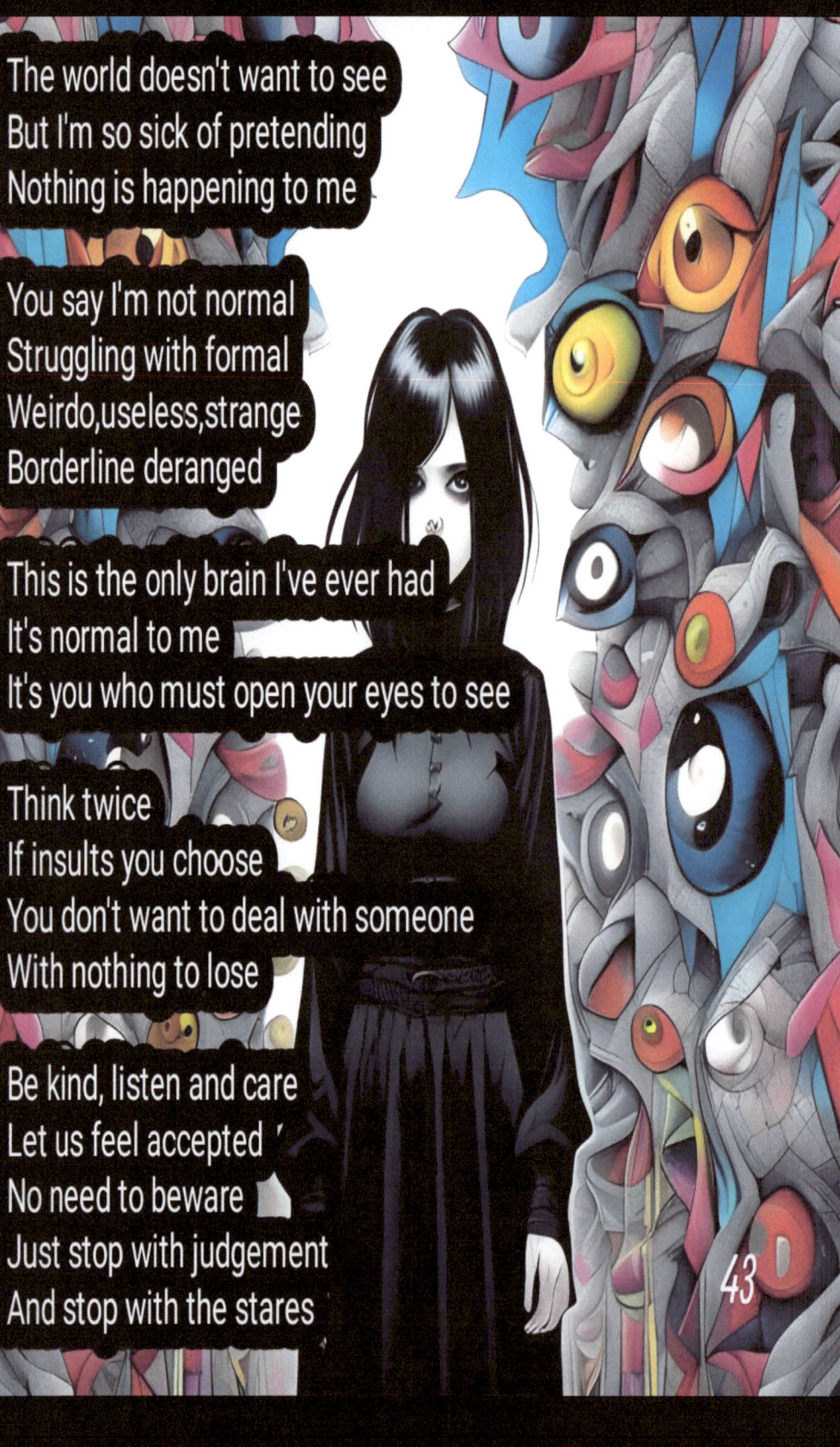

The world doesn't want to see
But I'm so sick of pretending
Nothing is happening to me

You say I'm not normal
Struggling with formal
Weirdo,useless,strange
Borderline deranged

This is the only brain I've ever had
It's normal to me
It's you who must open your eyes to see

Think twice
If insults you choose
You don't want to deal with someone
With nothing to lose

Be kind, listen and care
Let us feel accepted
No need to beware
Just stop with judgement
And stop with the stares

43

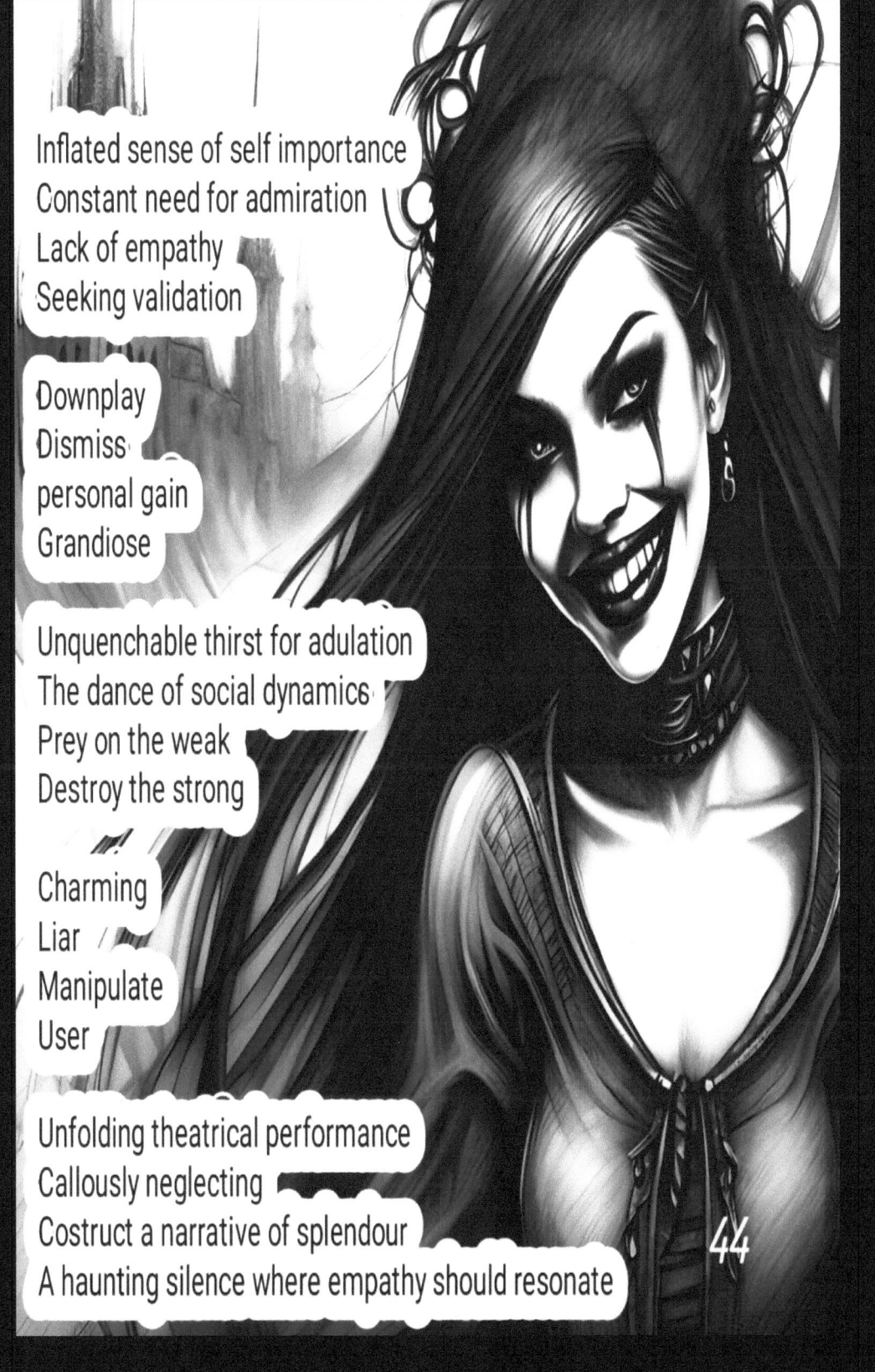

Inflated sense of self importance
Constant need for admiration
Lack of empathy
Seeking validation

Downplay
Dismiss
personal gain
Grandiose

Unquenchable thirst for adulation
The dance of social dynamics
Prey on the weak
Destroy the strong

Charming
Liar
Manipulate
User

Unfolding theatrical performance
Callously neglecting
Costruct a narrative of splendour
A haunting silence where empathy should resonate

44

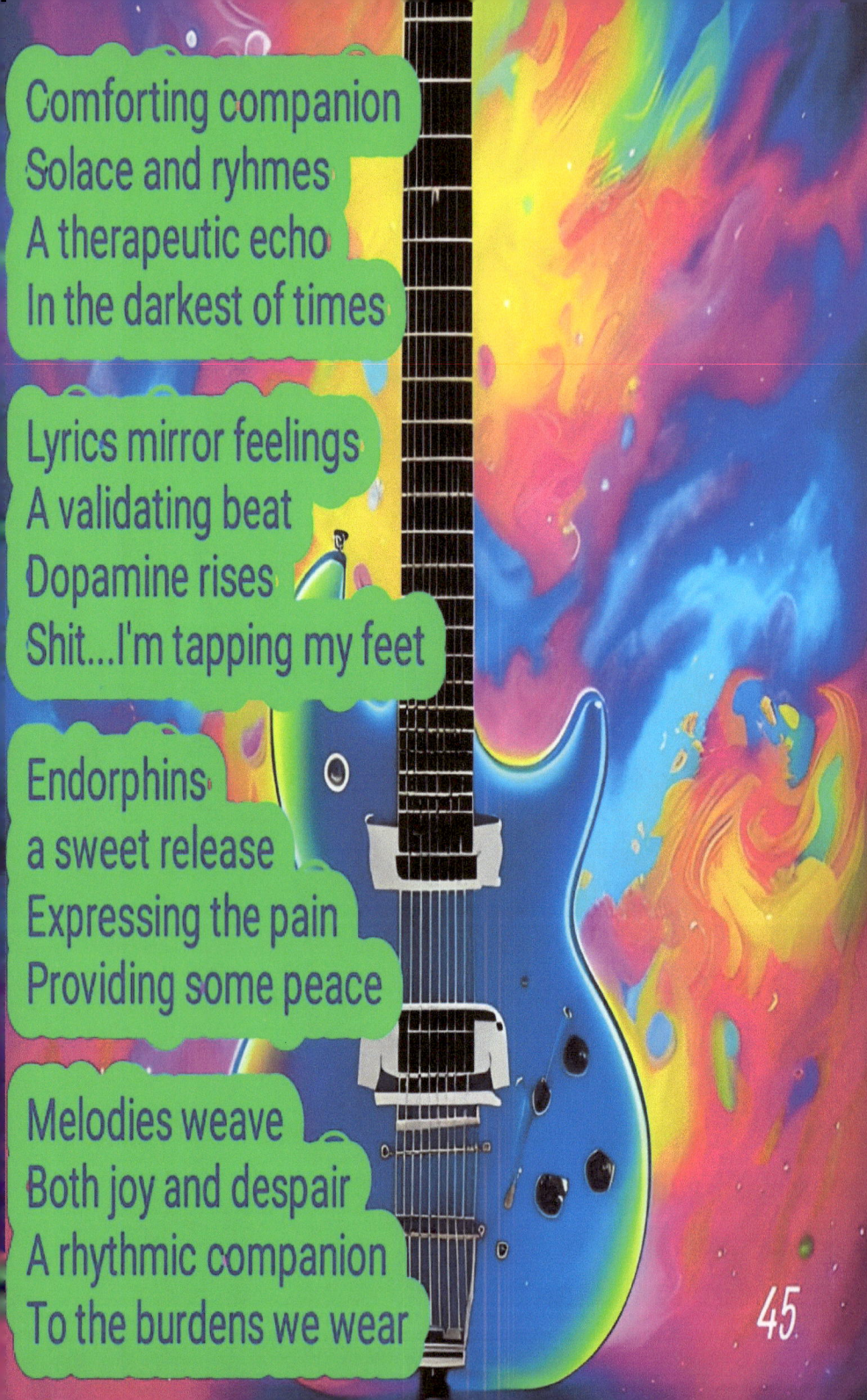

Comforting companion
Solace and ryhmes
A therapeutic echo
In the darkest of times

Lyrics mirror feelings
A validating beat
Dopamine rises
Shit....I'm tapping my feet

Endorphins
a sweet release
Expressing the pain
Providing some peace

Melodies weave
Both joy and despair
A rhythmic companion
To the burdens we wear

45

My poems might not be smart or complex
I might not have creative muscles to flex
Maybe I should stop and cease
But when it's about her
To me it's a masterpiece

With each syllable, a tribute I weave
In the simplicity, my love I conceive
I try to my best with poetic grace
Capturing the essence
Of her embrace

In the quiet cadence of my simple prose
I unravel the tale my heart bestows
No eloquent phrases
Just sentiment pure
Of reflection of my emotions
That forever endure

Open wide
Take your pill
Swallow it down
Suppress the pain
Make me palatable for your brain

Medical fortress
Made up of lies
Concealing the vulnerability
Behind my eyes

Bitterness lingers on the palate
Reminder of the pact
Sentinels of tranquity
This is all just an act

Scripted smiles
Chemical saga
Mental captor
How much longer
In this chemical chapter

47

You eyes burn bright
Melt the hearts of men
Don't get me confused
I'm not like them

I see through you
Makeup and tan
Could easily Seduce
A lesser man

You may burn
Your candle is bright
You disguise yourself
With the darkness of night

I won't engage
I don't want more
Your just the wax
You left on the floor

48

My journey has no
destination
Increase the distance
Between me and my
thoughts

It has no end

49

I love you so much
I love how you care
I love it when you
Stop and stare

You make me feel
Like I'm the best
Inferior to me
Are the rest

I love how you take
care of me
Show me how
great
Love can be

I could never hate
you
My heart is yours
I will never leave
You allow me
To finally breath

You don't do enough
Why don't you care
Stop looking at me
Stop with the stares

You've had better
I'm not the best
I'm inferior to the
rest

I don't like you
Fuck off already
Stop treating me
Like my minds
unsteady

You don't treat me
Like I'm normal
Just give me space
to breath

50

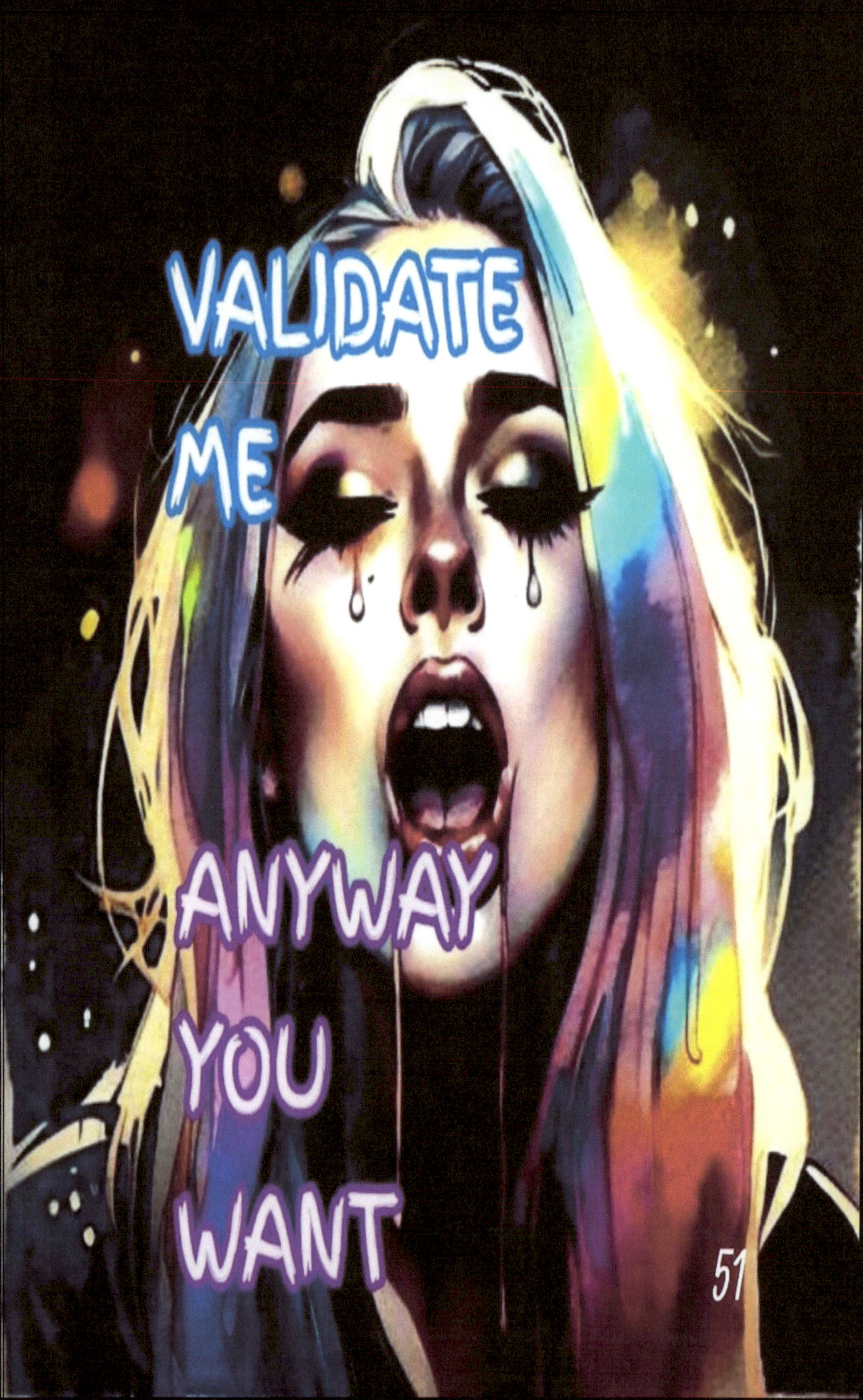
VALIDATE
ME
ANYWAY
YOU
WANT

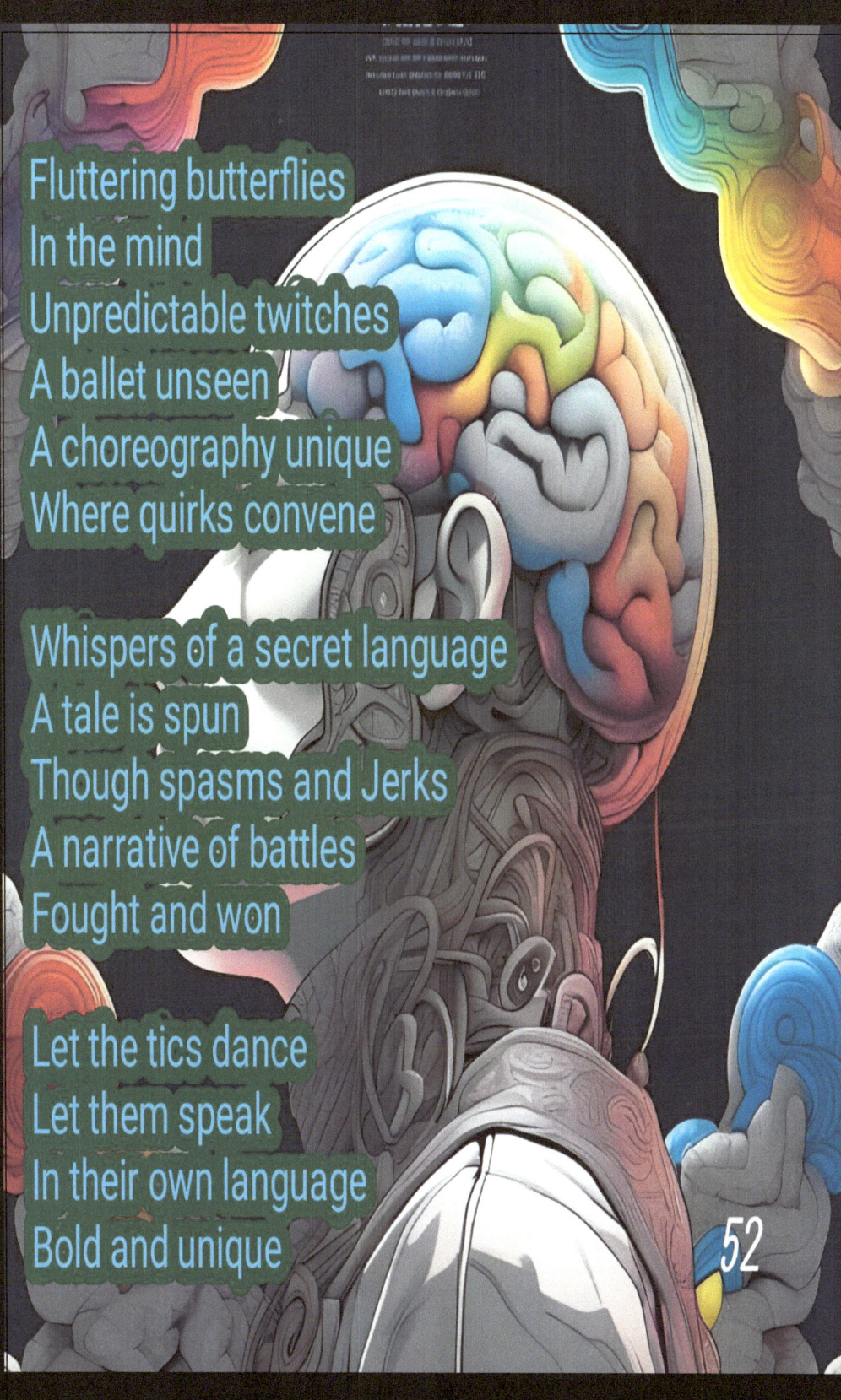

Fluttering butterflies
In the mind
Unpredictable twitches
A ballet unseen
A choreography unique
Where quirks convene

Whispers of a secret language
A tale is spun
Though spasms and Jerks
A narrative of battles
Fought and won

Let the tics dance
Let them speak
In their own language
Bold and unique

52

Boredom
Isolation
A dangerous mix
Anything
To get an emotional fix

A void to fill
Even though it won't fit
Just shove it in
A dopamine hit

Shopping
Shagging
Desperate nagging

Drinking
Pills and Degenerate thrills
Imaginary happiness
atop of that hill

Only to fall
A painful drop
This downward spiral
Doesn't seem to stop

On the long way down
Faces that laugh
Look what you did
Your life it total and utter shit

Looks like il climb that hill again
Why the fuck not
It's only my brain
That has started to rot

53

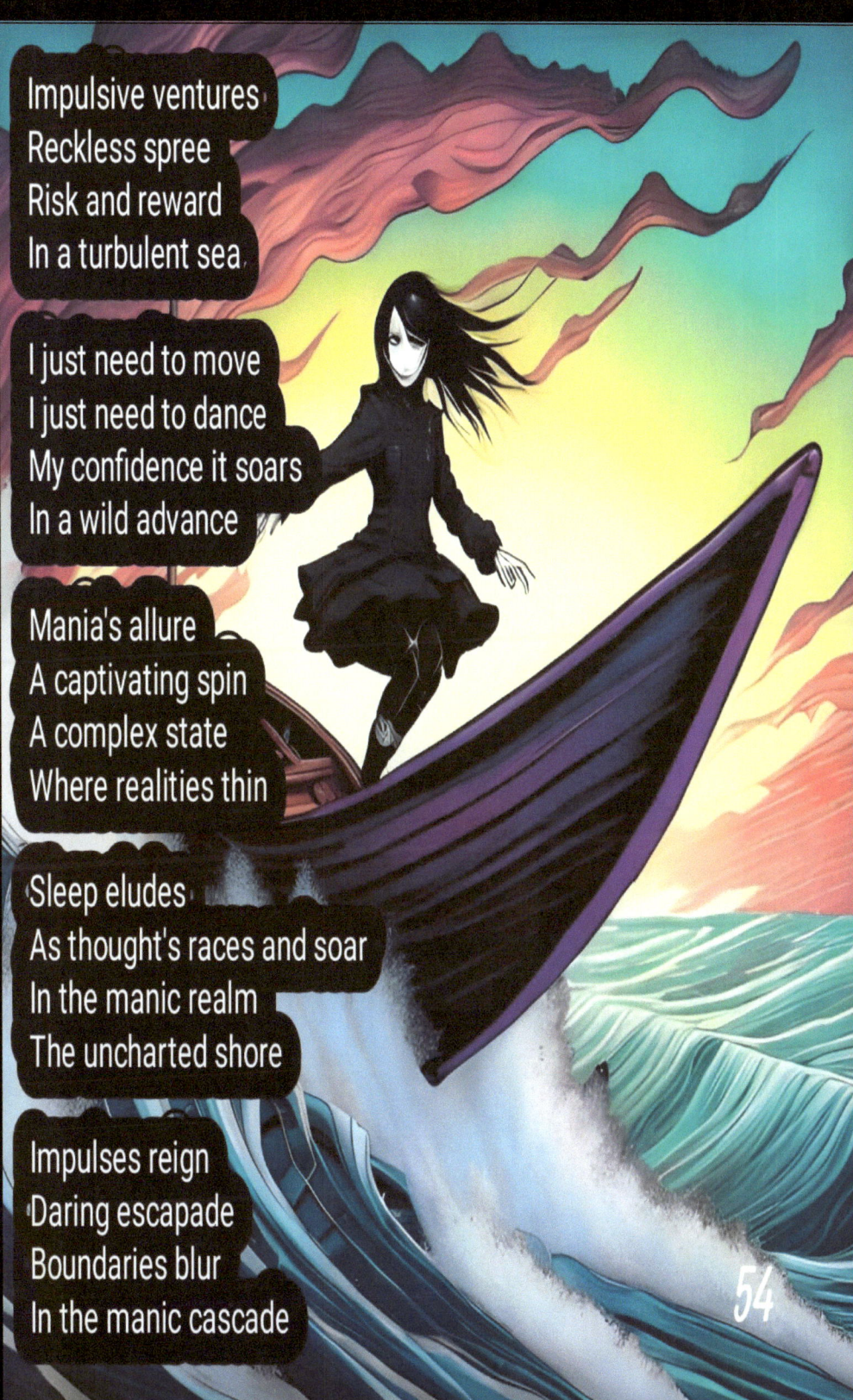

Impulsive ventures
Reckless spree
Risk and reward
In a turbulent sea.

I just need to move
I just need to dance
My confidence it soars
In a wild advance

Mania's allure
A captivating spin
A complex state
Where realities thin

Sleep eludes
As thought's races and soar
In the manic realm
The uncharted shore

Impulses reign
Daring escapade
Boundaries blur
In the manic cascade

54

Attention darts
From one to the other
The world around me
Feels like a series of distractions
Organisation
A daily struggle
Time feels slippery
Impulse to act
Overriding long term goals
A dance between spontaneity
Completing tasks
Feels like catching a fleeting thought
Concentrate slips away
Like sand through my fingers
Creativity overrides
Creating beauty in the chaos

55

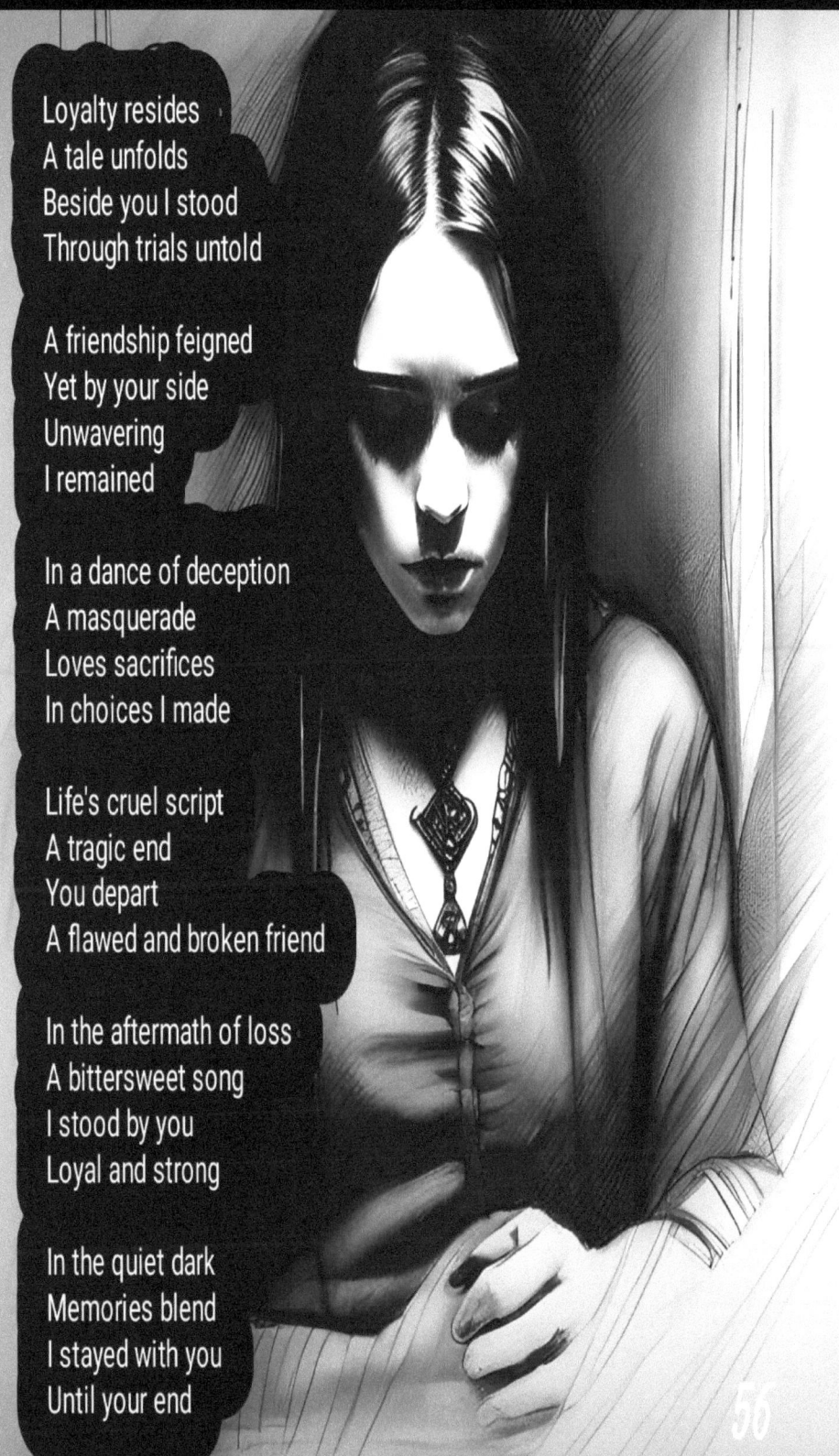

Loyalty resides
A tale unfolds
Beside you I stood
Through trials untold

A friendship feigned
Yet by your side
Unwavering
I remained

In a dance of deception
A masquerade
Loves sacrifices
In choices I made

Life's cruel script
A tragic end
You depart
A flawed and broken friend

In the aftermath of loss
A bittersweet song
I stood by you
Loyal and strong

In the quiet dark
Memories blend
I stayed with you
Until your end

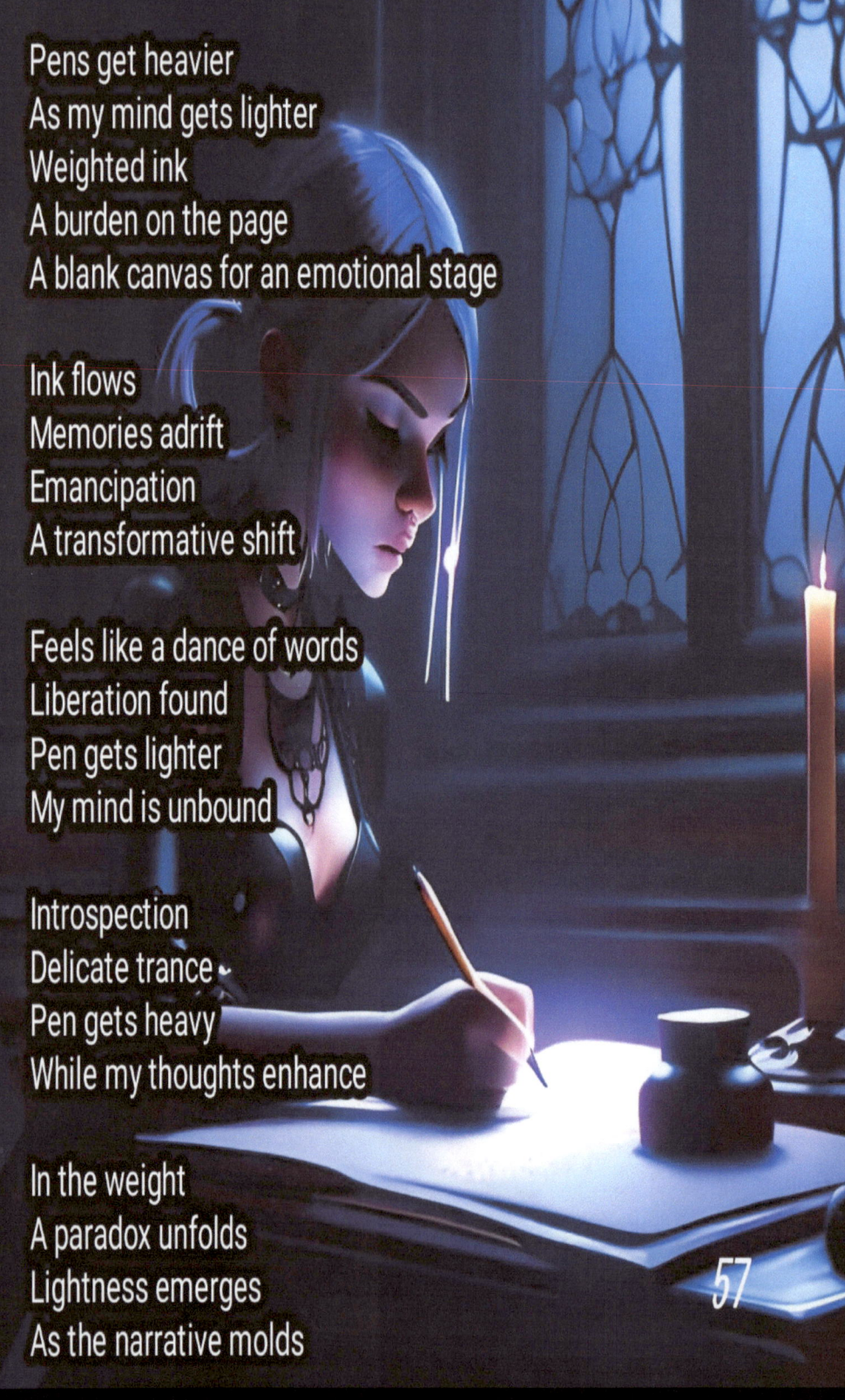

Pens get heavier
As my mind gets lighter
Weighted ink
A burden on the page
A blank canvas for an emotional stage

Ink flows
Memories adrift
Emancipation
A transformative shift

Feels like a dance of words
Liberation found
Pen gets lighter
My mind is unbound

Introspection
Delicate trance
Pen gets heavy
While my thoughts enhance

In the weight
A paradox unfolds
Lightness emerges
As the narrative molds

57

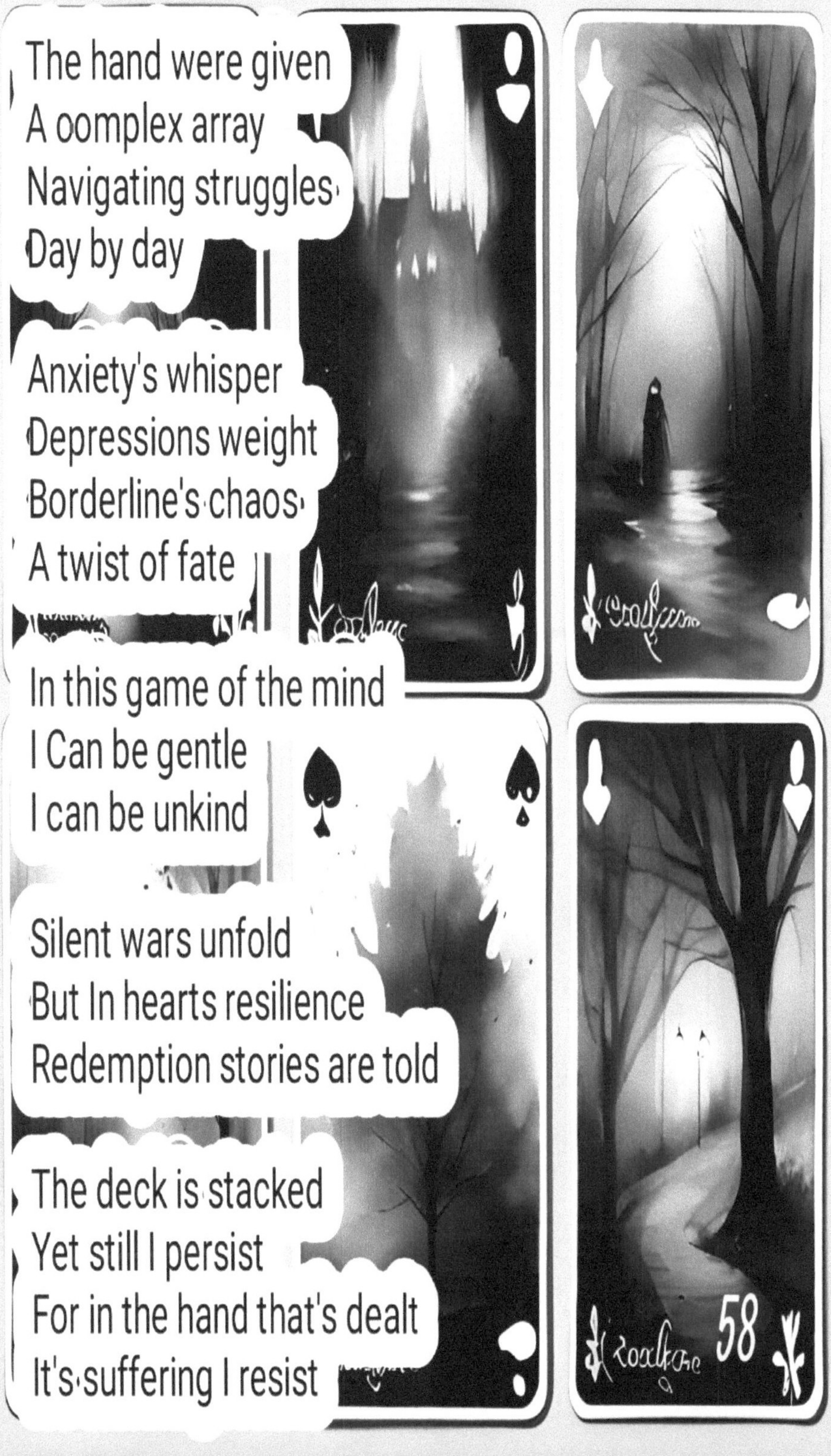

The hand were given
A oomplex array
Navigating struggles
Day by day

Anxiety's whisper
Depressions weight
Borderline's chaos
A twist of fate

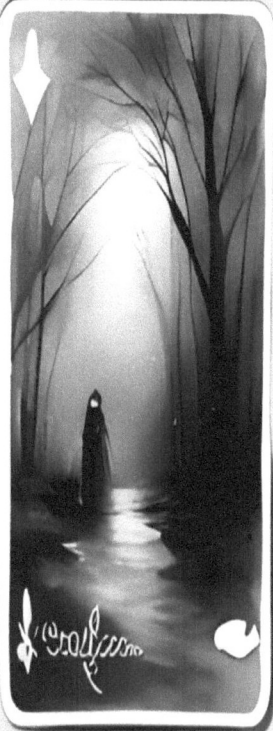

In this game of the mind
I Can be gentle
I can be unkind

Silent wars unfold
But In hearts resilience
Redemption stories are told

The deck is stacked
Yet still I persist
For in the hand that's dealt
It's suffering I resist

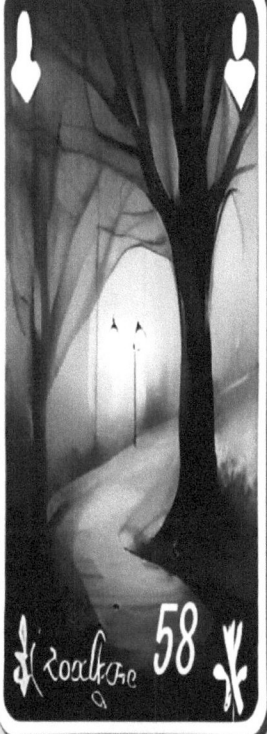

58

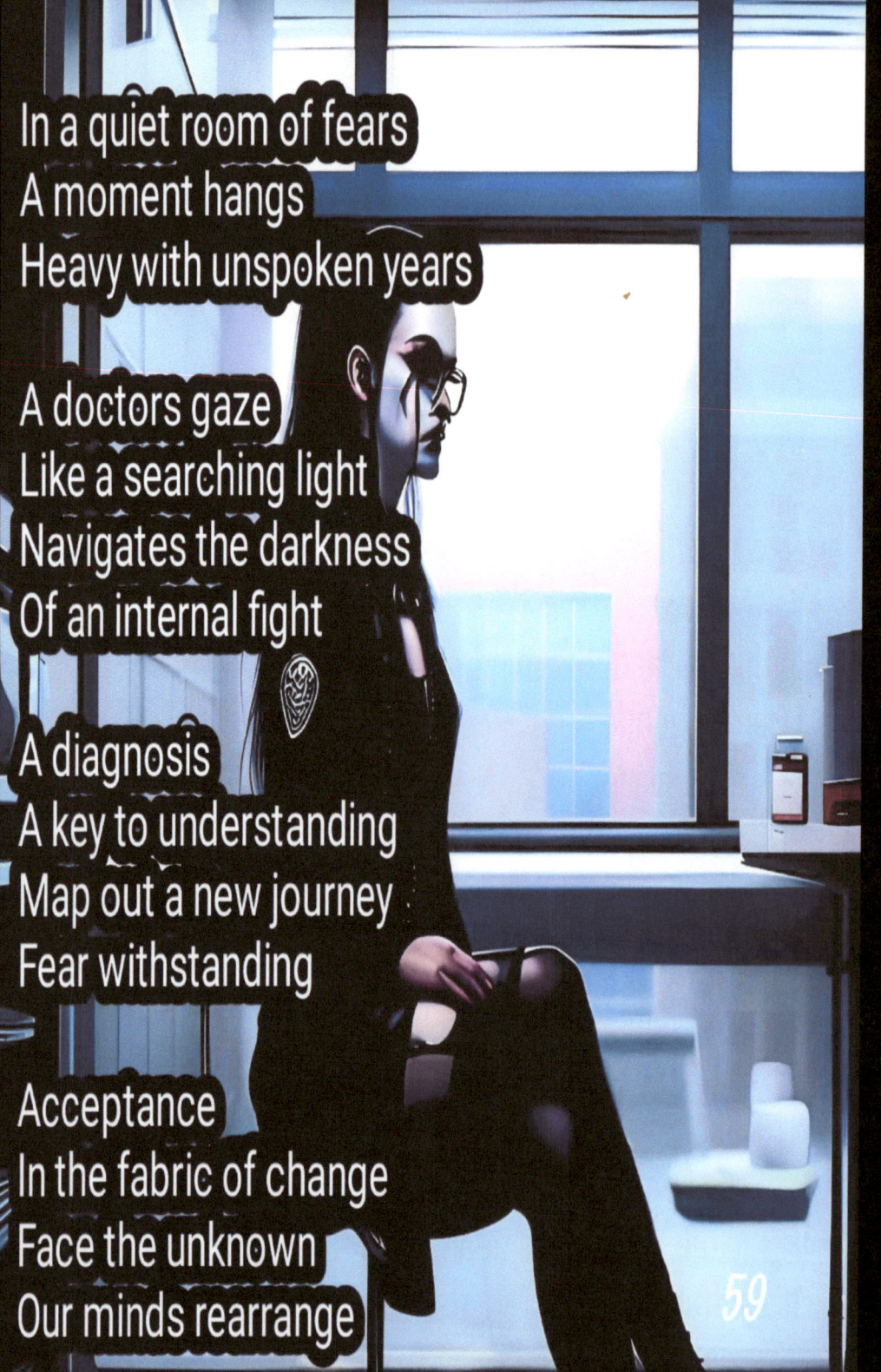

In a quiet room of fears
A moment hangs
Heavy with unspoken years

A doctors gaze
Like a searching light
Navigates the darkness
Of an internal fight

A diagnosis
A key to understanding
Map out a new journey
Fear withstanding

Acceptance
In the fabric of change
Face the unknown
Our minds rearrange

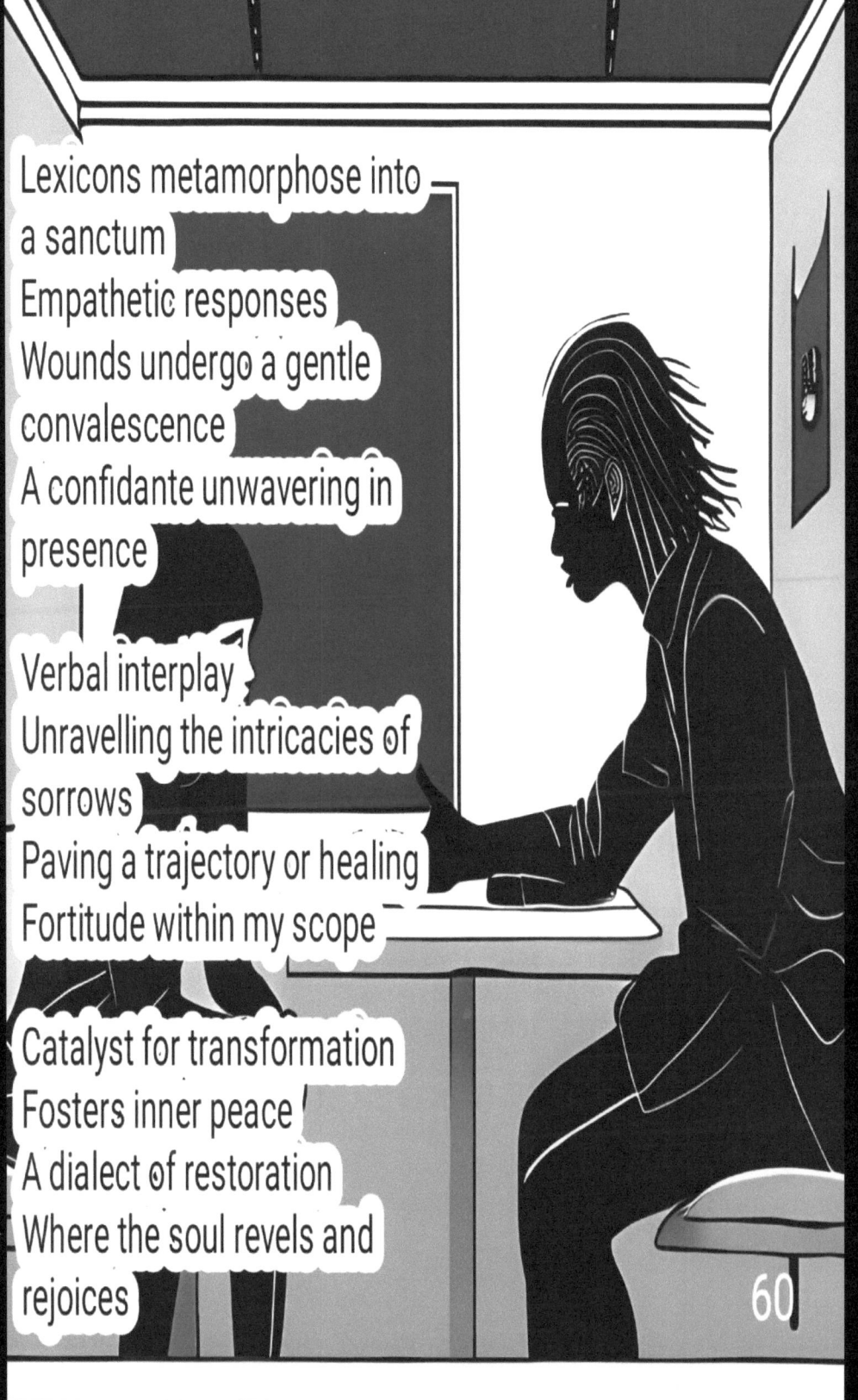

Lexicons metamorphose into a sanctum
Empathetic responses
Wounds undergo a gentle convalescence
A confidante unwavering in presence

Verbal interplay
Unravelling the intricacies of sorrows
Paving a trajectory or healing
Fortitude within my scope

Catalyst for transformation
Fosters inner peace
A dialect of restoration
Where the soul revels and rejoices

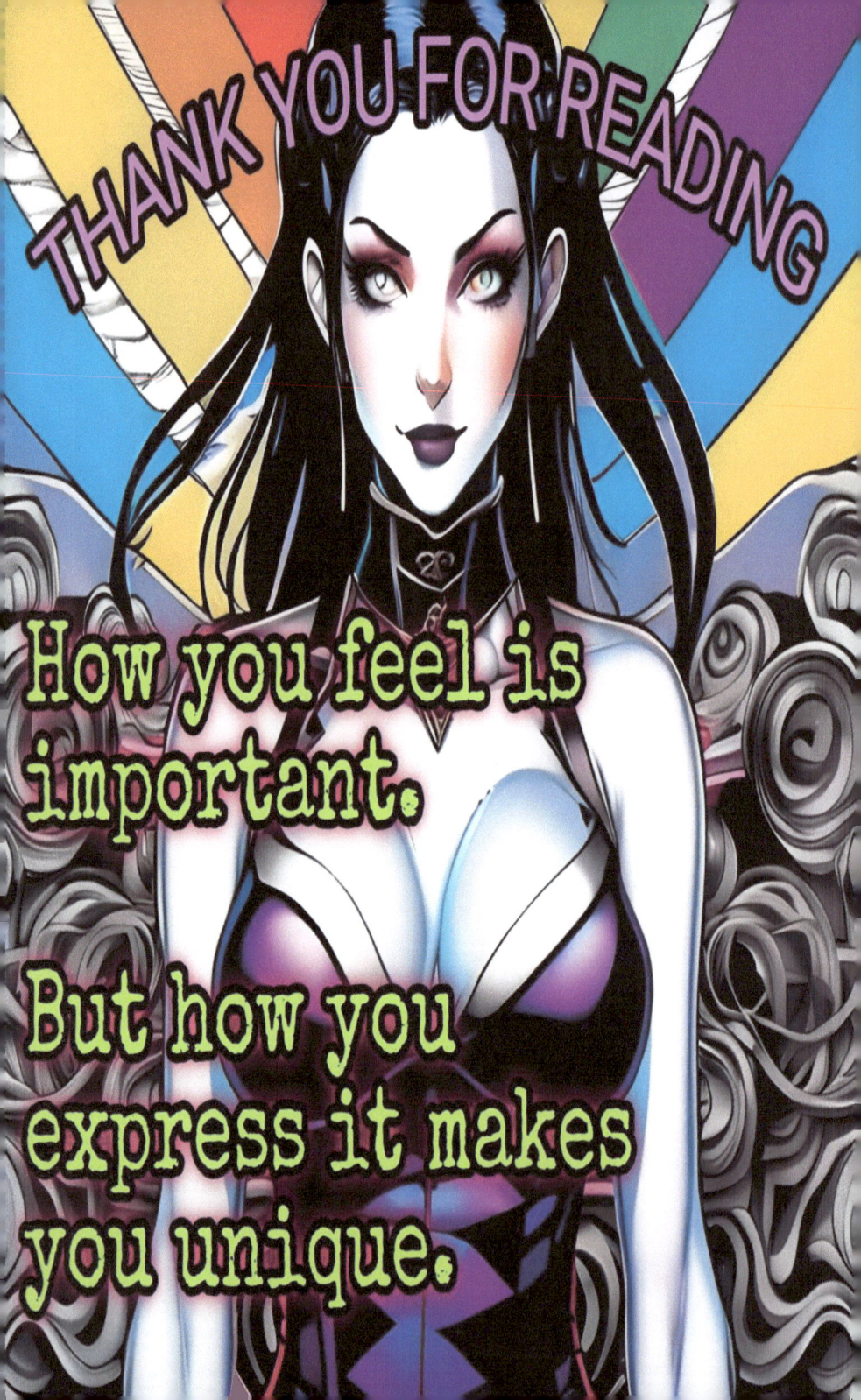

www.ingramcontent.com/pod-product-compliance
Lightning Source LLC
Chambersburg PA
CBHW050819290526
45792CB00001B/185